Am
The Kings

The Unknown Warrior
An Untold Story

Mark Scott

COLOURPOINT

Published 2020 by Colourpoint Books
an imprint of Colourpoint Creative Ltd
Colourpoint House, Jubilee Business Park
21 Jubilee Road, Newtownards, BT23 4YH
Tel: 028 9182 6339
E-mail: sales@colourpoint.co.uk
Web: www.colourpoint.co.uk

First Edition
First Impression

Text © Mark Scott, 2020
Illustrations © Various, as acknowledged in captions

All rights reserved. No part of this publication may be reproduced,
stored in a retrieval system or transmitted in any form or by any means, electronic,
mechanical, photocopying, scanning, recording or otherwise,
without the prior written permission of the copyright owners
and publisher of this book.

The author has asserted his right under the Copyright,
Designs and Patents Act, 1988, to be identified as author of this work.

A catalogue record for this book is available from the British Library.

Designed by April Sky Design, Newtownards
Tel: 028 9182 7195
Web: www.aprilsky.co.uk

Printed by GPS Colour Graphics Ltd, Belfast

ISBN 9781780732671

Front cover: A wreath of poppies at the Thiepval Memorial to the Missing, France.
Rear cover: (L) Rev. George Standing, Lt. Cecil Smith, Lt. Henry Williams and Maj.
Ernest Fitzsimon at St. Pol in 1920. (Author's collection)
(R) Maj. Fitzsimon at his brother Jack's grave in 1921, at Thiepval in France.
(Fitz-Simon family archive)

About the author: Mark Scott is a researcher with the Royal Ulster Rifles Museum
in Belfast. He was the author of *The Man Who Shot The Great War*, having previously
worked as research consultant for the Doubleband Films/BBC film documentary
of the same name which aired November 2014. Mark recently taught photography
at Queen's University in Belfast, a subject which he continues to pursue and enjoy
while researching battlefield sites throughout the world.

Scott's conclusion is that they received a proper burial in a British Cemetery alongside their brothers in arms.

At the end of his eight year journey researching Jimmy Scott's notebook, having visited many of the relatives of those named in the notebook, Mark had one last duty to perform. He applied for Jack Fitzsimons' medals that his mother had refused to accept in 1920 and had them despatched to Jack's great niece. This was a particularly thoughtful and compassionate conclusion to his research into his great grandfather's notebook recording the names of his friends and colleagues killed in the service of their country in 1916.

Mark Scott's book is a very detailed and important record of those Royal Irish Riflemen who fought in the Great War with his great grandfather.

General Sir Roger Wheeler GCB, CBE
May 2020

Prologue
France, April 2012

THE EARLY MORNING flight from Belfast descended through thick grey cloud to touch down at a dull grey Paris Charles De Gaulle airport. The passengers sprang into motion as the aircraft taxied to a standstill, engaging in the struggle from their seats to the exit door, dislodging precariously stowed cases and belongings from the overhead lockers en route. I followed on, trance-like, in line with other grey people into the bowels of the airport, my thought interrupted occasionally with splashes of vibrant red, blue and bright yellow as excited children broke loose from the airport protocols, fuelled with excitement in anticipation of an impending Disney visit dressed as their favourite character, only to be pulled back into line by stressed parents.

After an age of administration, waiting and form-filling, I eventually walked out into the Paris light to complete my journey by hire car. The morning felt more winter than spring, cold, damp and grey as I negotiated my way out of the circular grey maze of the airport, eventually leaving behind the furious taxi drivers, unaccustomed to my lack of knowledge of an exit to the Autoroute Du Nord, an escape route to the countryside.

I progressed carefully, constantly working my mind to tune into the local driving techniques while keeping a count of the exit numbers, almost becoming complacent until jolted by the realisation that I had to turn off onto smaller roads and pass into rural France. As beams of sunlight began to penetrate the cloud I passed signs of villages that meant little to me then, Carnoy, Mametz, Fricourt, La Boisselle, before decelerating to take the sharp turn at Aveluy in the direction of Thiepval. That name I did know something about, hardly enough then, but the name was familiar. There had been an horrific battle there, it was where the Ulstermen made their mark in history. However, Thiepval was not my final destination.

I drove for a short distance along the bank of the River Ancre. I could not see the river but knew from the map that I had with me that it was there, slowly moving behind dense trees to my left. In the distance a church spire could be seen just as I approached the sign that marked the edge of the village that was my destination, Authuille. I passed a French cemetery on my left then one or two low bungalows, furnished in traditional red brick with red tiled roofs typical with elaborate motifs of fancy brickwork framing the edges of the doors and windows. There was not a person to be seen.

A dark green sign with white lettering indicated that I turn left, downhill on a narrow road in the direction of the river. After about 100 metres the road turned sharply right across the front of a long low building; a short patch of road, more akin to a driveway, branched off left and stopped at a green grass pathway. Here, I stopped, mindful that I may have parked on someone's property, and stepped out of the car. A light mist immediately shrouded me and the cold penetrated my clothing as I made my way downhill on the perfectly manicured grass pathway; ahead, at the end of the dew-covered grass I was met by a wall and gateway behind which loomed the Cross Of Sacrifice, a seven metre high cross made of Portland stone faced with a bronze longsword mounted blade pointing down, indicating a Commonwealth War Graves Commission cemetery containing more than forty graves. I had arrived at Authuile British Cemetery.

Only after I clunked open the heavy gate latch and walked down the steps beside the Great Cross did I see the grave stones themselves, formed up in lines along the bank running parallel with the river below. The light mist had dampened any sound save for the steady bubbling trickle of water still out of sight beyond the far boundary. This was the most peaceful of places. A tranquility suddenly enveloped me in stark contrast to the bustle of plane, airport and traffic that had occupied my mind up to that point. I pushed my hand into my jacket pocket where it reassuringly found the cover of a small leather-bound diary and I began to walk among the graves of the fallen, scanning the names and regimental badges carved into the white stones, looking for those I had learnt just the day before. Without realising, I had passed the start of the row that I had sought. I turned to face the men, drew the little notebook from my pocket and turned the fragile, crisp pages until I found the page marked with the pencil notes 'Authuille (nr Martinsart) killed night of 5th May'. I read down a list, at each name I looked up, almost as in a response to a call of the roll my eyes met the corresponding name in stone: Lieutenant Walker, Privates Beattie, McBratney, Martin, Adams, Sloane, McKeown, Lance Corporal Lowe and Private Tollerton. Each grave bore the badge of The Royal Irish Rifles, each with the same date of death, the 6th May 1916.

The notebook had belonged to my great grandfather James (Jimmy) Scott. These were his men, he was their Sergeant in the 14th Royal Irish Rifles, a battalion known as The Young Citizen Volunteers. As I stood there in the early spring chill a thought struck hard inside me that on a similar morning in May 1916 he stood at or close to the very spot where I was and noted in the book which I held the names of his dead comrades, the names I had just read out. At that moment I vowed to discover as much as I could about these men and others named in two sections of the book. In the years that followed that promise led me to new friendships, family members I hadn't known, discovering photographs unseen for a century and uncovering the stories and lives of those who gave their all in the Great War. It led me to the writing of a book following research that contributed to a television documentary, *The Man Who Shot The Great War* and to many visits to the battlefields where men like Jimmy Scott played out their final minutes.

Juxtaposed with the extraordinary deeds of seemingly ordinary people I discovered that one Ulsterman played a key part in an operation that secured and preserved the remembrance of thousands of missing men who were denied a grave through the misfortunes of war. This man played a part in a scheme whereby the focus of grieving, remembrance, and the acceptance of sacrifice of millions of people were realised. His story, and my connections to him follows. Through his efforts and the foresight of others,

Their Name Liveth
For Evermore.

1

A Notebook

THE NOTEBOOK IN my pocket was actually a pre-printed 1916 diary. It was small, smaller than a packet of cigarettes and less than half as thin. It was bound with a mottled black leather cover that looped at the rear cover edge to form a little sheath for an accompanying pencil. The pencil, still attached, was tiny, of about the same size as a three inch nail, just big enough to use between finger and thumb. The little pencil was coated in a light blue enamel and was finished at the top with a metal cap, formed with a protruding lip to enable it to be easily removed with a thumbnail from the tight grip of the leather sheath. The pencil had obviously been sharpened by hand using a knife of some kind to reveal about an eighth of an inch of lead protruding from the roughly cut light wood. I held the whole simple system of recording in my hand, the pencil and the book protecting gold gilt-edged pages with their priceless content.

The cover of the book was embossed in gold with the insignia of the New Zealand Shipping Company along with an extract from Shakesphere's famous St. Crispin's Day speech from the play Henry V. Inside the front cover in the owner's handwriting was written, James Scott, 32 Elm Street, Donegall Pass, Belfast, Ireland and on the page opposite the following details: 15892 Sergeant James Scott, 14th Royal Irish Rifles, 'B' Company, No. 7 Platoon. The date of this entry was recorded as the 26th February 1916. On the 26th February 1916 the 14th Battalion of the Royal Irish Rifles was deployed[1] with the British Expeditionary Force (B.E.F.)

---

1 14th R.I.R. War Diary, R.U.R. Museum.

close to an expanding railway hub near Varennes in France, built to ensure that all of the various ingredients for the then coming 'big push' could be assembled and moved up to the front line storage dumps. Jimmy Scott and No. 7 platoon had been employed as labourers working for the Royal Engineers in the railway construction.

By the time he took possession of the little diary in February 1916 Jimmy Scott had been in service with the 14th Royal Irish Rifles for almost eighteen months from the date the battalion was formed on 12th September 1914. Even then though, back at the beginning of the war, he was an old soldier. He had served for four years as a regular soldier with the 2nd Royal Irish Fusiliers having lied about his age on the day of his attestation on the 12th October 1898. The white lie added a year to his actual age and facilitated his recruitment to The Colours. The same lie also had the effect of partly relieving the burden on his parents of feeding and clothing his eleven siblings in their small cottage at Tullyhue, County Armagh. Practically the whole family were employed in the nearby Sinton's Mill. Jimmy made a decision at the age of 17 to exchange the hold of the mill and the predictable, harsh life that it held in store for one of uncertainty and adventure.

Just over a year later that adventure began when Jimmy found himself on active service in South Africa. The army had trained him and schooled him and on the 23rd October 1899[2] he set sail with his battalion from Southampton on board the *Howarden Castle*, bound for Cape Town. Jimmy Scott kept a diary for the most part of his service during the Boer War in South Africa. The original was in his own handwriting although the vocabulary used is not representative of that used by a 17 year old Armagh mill worker. When researching the document a similar, almost word for word identical diary was discovered in the collection of the Royal Irish Fusiliers Museum in Armagh. The Armagh version however belonged

---

2 Personal Diary, James Scott, Scott Family Archive.

to a drummer in the same battalion called Barton. One theory put up for the two near-identical documents was that both Jimmy Scott and drummer Barton and perhaps other junior soldiers were instructed to copy an officer's journal as part of their educational training. Whatever the explanation for the near duplication of the two documents we are left with a comprehensive diary of events of his service during the Boer war. There is no doubt that his South Africa service placed him in a position of high regard among his new army recruits of 1914. He was one of only three men in the battalion to have previously been under enemy fire and knew to a certain extent what serving in a foreign land would entail. His previous service ensured an appointment to Sergeant rank in the new battalion and a role in instructing the new recruits, fresh from civilian life in the ways of the army.

Jimmy Scott's first tastes of the changing fortunes of war came about from the attempts of the British forces to break the siege of Ladysmith. On the 15th December 1899 the 2nd Royal Irish Fusiliers were attached to the 6th Fusilier Brigade under Major General Geoffrey Barton. The brigade was named the 'Union' Brigade as it was made from fusilier battalions from England, Scotland, Wales and Ireland. The brigade was involved in its first major engagement of the war in trying to unseat the Boer forces from defensive positions at Colenso; doing so would open the way to the relief of the besieged town of Ladysmith. Jimmy Scott described the battle as follows:[3]

> 'A day that will not be forgotten by those who took part in this battle. We did not know we were going into action until the Boers opened fire with Pom-Poms and Mausers etc. We struck camp at 2.30am, had breakfast at 3.15am and marched off at 4am. Four companies under Colonel Reeves going as escort to the naval guns and the other four companies with the Brigade. We did not advance

3 Ibid.

very far before the roar of the enemy's canon told us we were in for a very hot day's work. The naval guns got into action at once. The Boers replying from three or four different positions, both sides making splendid shooting. About 6am the infantry moved out in battle formation. It seemed as if we were marching into a wall of fire as the Boers kept up a terrific fire. The order of advance was as follows. The Irish Brigade under General Hart on the left. The Fusilier Brigade on the right under General Barton. The Rifle Brigade and English Brigades under Generals Lyttleton and Hildyard advanced in centre of the line towards Colenso Bridge.

'The Irish Brigade were the first to lose heavily. As General Hart moved them up in close formation the enemy profited only too well with this chance and opened fire on the heroic Irishmen. The men of the brigade fell in dozens but thanks to their splendid courage they deployed out the same as if they were drilling on the barracks square.

'The day was well advanced by this time. The heat was unbearable and we could get no water to wet our parched mouths with. It seemed the day would never end. Men and horses fell in all directions. So after ten hours hard fighting we were obliged to retire with a loss of 447 killed, wounded or missing. Also ten guns lost.'

Jimmy Scott had survived what became known as 'Black Week'. The defeat at Colenso was the third British defeat by the Boers in a space of five days. Three days later Jimmy entered a short note into his diary that related to a specific incident during the battle:

'18th, Outpost duty. Lord Robert's son died of wounds received in action on the 15th when trying to save the guns.'

During the battle two batteries of field guns of the 14th and 66th Batteries, Royal Field Artillery under the command

until April 1901 Jimmy was based at Machadodorf on the
Elands River. His duties here comprised occasional patrols
and periods of manning blockhouses, constructed to protect
main supply routes. His diary entries became few and far
between; typically an entry would begin with the words
'Still at Machadodorf'. It would appear that Jimmy Scott
had succumbed to that always near companion of a soldier,
boredom. Then on the 6th April 1901 he had an opportunity
to break the monotony and wrote:

> 'It came out in orders that there were 64 men wanted for
> the Mounted Infantry so I volunteered and we were all
> sent away on the 6th for Pretoria. When we arrived in it
> we were sent to the M.I. Depot just by the Race Course
> and we got our saddlery. We were here three days and
> then we were sent up to Daspoort Camp where we got
> our horses. We had three parades per day in the menage.
> We were not here long until we could fairly twill on
> the gee-gee's back. We stopped here for a fortnight and
> on the 23rd we were sent down to Standerton to join
> Goughs Mounted on Colonel Bullocks column. We got
> to the column which was lying about 1/2 mile out of the
> town and as soon as we arrived there we had to fall in at
> once and go and draw remounts from the remount depot
> as the column was going on the trek the next morning
> at 5 o'clock.'

On the 24th April 1901 Jimmy Scott makes his last entry
in his diary:

> 'We go out towards Blauwkop. The Boers are very active
> round here sniping all day at the rear guard.'

It is interesting to note that his form of English language
used in these later entries differed considerably from those
previously entered, as though we are reading his own words,
not those dictated or copied from an officer's journal. This
shows us perhaps that a level of education had been attained
and that although that by volunteering for the Mounted

Infantry he detached himself from his tutor, Jimmy had gained a level of confidence in literacy to continue to make his own entries. At this point the diary also differs from that of drummer Barton, indicating that the two men had followed different paths. All this said, no further diary entries were made by Jimmy Scott. An explanation for this may be that they were frowned upon by his new officers. Being involved in the mobile warfare carried out by the Mounted Infantry meant a higher chance of becoming isolated and captured. If this were to happen and the diary was seized by the Boers, any previous day's entries could provide vital intelligence to the enemy. It could have been the case that the diary was left at base while he took part on long treks and patrols.

The theory of not recording details for fear of capture was, in the case of Jimmy Scott, proven to have been a good enough reason not to keep a diary. On the 17th September 1901 Major Gough's 24th Mounted Infantry numbering 585 men observed a Boer Commando of around 300 men resting at Sheepers Nek at Blood River Poort. These men were unsaddled and resting at the foot of a small hill. Gough believed he had the element of surprise and decided to attack the Boer unit without any further reconnaissance. The attack involved a charge of over a mile at full gallop. Gough had not known that the majority of the Boer unit numbering some 700 men on horseback were actually making their way towards him, out of sight around the hill, just at the time he ordered the charge. They quickly encircled Gough's men and after a short but fierce fight Gough was forced to surrender a group of around 250 men. The remainder of his force scattered and those who were able made their way back to the nearest British base at Vryheid some 25 miles away.

Major Gough himself was captured but later escaped from the Boers. Private Jimmy Scott, service no. 6322, was also among those taken prisoner. The Boer General commanding directed that the prisoners, far from being shot or harmed in any way, be simply stripped of all uniform, equipment and horses and set free to walk the 25 miles back to Vryheid. Thus Jimmy Scott, although humiliated, survived the defeat. The commander of the Boer forces at Blood River Poort on that day was Commandant General Louis Botha. Botha went on to become the first Prime Minister of The Union of South Africa, the forerunner of the modern South Africa state. He later became a British ally and assisted in fighting the German forces in West Africa during the Great War. News of Jimmy Scott's involvement in the incident was published in the *Belfast News Letter*[5] where he was initially reported as 'missing'. A few days later a second report confirmed that he had been captured and released, the Boers having been unable to retain prisoners of war due to their mobile guerrilla style of combat at that time. The second Boer War, as it was known, ended on the 31st May 1902 when the Boer leadership accepted terms of surrender and signed the Treaty of Vereeniging. Jimmy Scott remained in South Africa for a few months following the surrender until he recorded a footnote in his diary that stated:

> 'Set sail from Capetown SA on the 5th October 1902 and arrived at Southampton on 27th October on board the Arundle Castle.'

A month later, on the 27th November 1902 Jimmy Scott transferred from regular military service to the reserve meaning that he could live and work as a civilian but remained on the army's books to be recalled to service if required. He remained on the army reserve for eight years until 1910.

On the 10th September 1912 Jimmy joined an organisation in Belfast called the Young Citizen Volunteers of Ireland, later known as the Young Citizen Volunteers or simply Y.C.V. The concept of the Young Citizen Volunteers had been hatched from as early as 6th June 1912 when meetings were held

---

5 *Belfast News Letter*, 'The Mishap to Gough's Force' 19/9/1901

by the Financial Committee of the Young Citizen Volunteers presided over by the Lord Mayor, Robert James McMordie at Belfast City Hall. An article published on that date in the *Belfast News Letter*[6] announced as follows:

'YOUNG CITIZENS' VOLUNTEER CORPS
Meeting in the City Hall.

A most interesting meeting was held in the Lord Mayor's parlour yesterday afternoon when a number of prominent citizens met on the invitation of the Lord Mayor to consider the proposal to form a "Young Citizens' Volunteer Corps." The Lord Mayor, who presided, expressed his anxiety to associate himself with any movement calculated to assist in the intellectual and physical development of the young men of Belfast, and with this object he had invited the gentlemen present to consider the proposals put before him by Mr. F.T. Geddis, whom he then called upon to address the meeting. Mr. Geddis briefly outlined his scheme, emphasising the fact that the most critical period in a young man's life was after he had reached the age of eighteen, and urging that some effort should be made to form a non-political and non-sectarian organisation, having for its objects:-

The development of a manly physique by means of modified military and police drill including development of a spirit of responsible citizenship on the part of our young men by means of lectures on civic matters, such as the size and population of one's native town or city, its public boards and their functions, it's public men and their work, its past history etc and (2) The development of a manly physique by means of modified military and police drill including free gymnastics, single-stick, bayonet and baton exercises, swimming, compass-reading, signalling (hand, flag and flashlight), ambulance work etc. The Lord

---

6 *Belfast News Letter*, 'Young Citizen's Volunteer Corps Meeting in the City Hall' 6/6/1912

Mayor said he considered the scheme an excellent one, and asked for an expression of opinion from those present. This was freely given, the following gentlemen, amongst others, expressing their approval:- Major Crawford, Major Cunningham, Lieutenant Colonel W.E.C. McCammond, J.P.; Messrs W. Joseph Stokes; G.W. Ferguson, J.P.; E.J. Elliott, J.E. Dawson, E.M Reid and Councillor Dr. Williamson, the latter gentleman laying special emphasis on the importance of ambulance work.'

Further meetings were held until the inauguration in Belfast on the 10th September 1912. A constitution and set of rules had been agreed and adopted along with a rank structure following the lines of section, company and battalion strengths. Each company was to number between 30 and 50 men and be under the command of a Captain. Each company was to have a Lieutenant to every 25 men and one Staff Sergeant to every section of 10 men. Jimmy Scott was chosen to be part of this organisation from its inception. He was appointed Staff Sergeant and began to train the young men in his section, drawing on his own military training and experience.

Throughout 1913 a number of requests were made to the government in London to provide military equipment and indeed 'surplus' weapons to enable the Young Citizen Volunteers to drill and train in a military fashion. The political climate in Belfast at this time was beginning to heat up with Ulster Volunteer Force Battalions taking steps to arm themselves using smuggled weapons in reaction to the proposed imposition of Home Rule to Ireland by the Westminster Government. Needless to say the requests to arm the Y.C.V. from London fell upon deaf ears as the Government of the day would not back or recognise any official 'territorial' unit. At this time Jimmy Scott was working as a tram conductor with the Belfast Tramway Company, part of the Belfast Corporation. He had previously been working as an agent for the MacNaughton cement company at Waring Street in Belfast which entailed him driving deliveries across Northern Ireland. He had married Jane Thompson on Christmas Day 1908 with her brother, Robert Thompson attending the wedding as Best Man. Robert Thompson also worked along with Jimmy as a tram conductor and lodged with him and Jane at their house at 32 Elm Street, off Donegall Pass in Belfast. On joining the Y.C.V. in September 1912 James and Jane had four children with a fifth on the way. Jimmy, Jane and family are pictured together in a photograph taken in the studio of Robert Lyttle at Dublin Road, Belfast around September 1912. James can be seen wearing a Young Citizen Volunteer lapel badge.

The Young Citizen Volunteers recruited mainly from the 'better off' of Belfast's young men. Monthly dues were required to be paid and their exclusive uniform had to be purchased by the members from their own funds. There were differences in quality, fit and shade depending on where the uniform was tailored and how much was spent on it. The uniform itself was light grey in colour with navy blue collar and cuffs, reminiscent of an American 'West Point' officer cadet's uniform. The officers had an open neck tunic with shirt and tie and Sergeant Majors' uniform differed again with embroidered edges on the stand-up collar. On the shoulder epaulettes 'Y.C.V.' lettering was worn along with the number '1' denoting the 1st Battalion. It was originally envisaged that there would be four battalions recruited from each of the provinces of Ireland. This ambitious idea never came to fruition. The cap badge depicted a shamrock surmounted by a crown with a hand of Ulster in the centre.

As 1913 passed by the fear of home rule being imposed increased amongst Ulstermen. James was placed under extreme personal pressure. He had divided loyalties. His military experience was needed to train and drill the Y.C.V. However he was also a member of the South Belfast Ulster

1914 was fighting in yet another battle, this time it was at La Bassée. It was to be his last. He was evacuated from the front lines after receiving gunshot wounds to his left arm and thigh, shipped back to England and was admitted to the Nottingham General Hospital on the 30th October 1914 for treatment. Corporal Robert Elphick died of his wounds at 7.55am on the morning of the 7th November 1914. R.S.M. Robert Elphick remained with the Y.C.V. throughout their training at Finner, Randalstown in County Antrim and Seaford in East Sussex, deploying with the Battalion and his remaining son, Ernest, who had been promoted to Corporal, to France on October 6th 1915. Both men were eventually returned from front line duties under medical grounds. Ernest was discharged from the Army due to 'sickness' on the 7th June 1916. His father, Robert was transferred from front line duties in France on the 12th May 1916 suffering from lumbago. He continued to serve in a training role until he finally left the military on the 27th March 1919. In addition to receiving his 1914–15 Star, British War and Victory Medals he was mentioned in War Office Communique of 28th August 1919 for 'Valuable services rendered in connection with the war'. He was 51 years of age. Robert John Elphick passed away at his home at Stockmans Lane in Belfast on the 13th May 1941, aged 72 years. He was immortalised by the acclaimed Irish artist and official war artist William Conor who made a portrait of him in pastels. It is permanently on display in the Royal Ulster Rifles Museum in Belfast.

During the heady days of enlistment, recruitment and training of new battalions Jimmy Scott harboured similar concerns for family members to Sergeant Major Elphick. At the outbreak of war his next youngest brother William had been serving as a regular soldier in the 2nd Battalion of The Royal Inniskilling Fusiliers. He had deployed to fight in France and Flanders on the 23rd August 1914 with the British Expeditionary Force (B.E.F.) 4th Division with the

2nd Inniskillings forming part of the 12th Infantry Brigade. Having initially been held in reserve the 4th Division were thrown into what was to become known as The Retreat From Mons. By the time the newly formed 14th Royal Irish Rifles had all been sworn in for service on the 14th September 1914 the 2nd Royal Inniskilling Fusiliers had lost 60 men killed or missing with over 200 wounded. William Scott was soon wounded himself and was returned home in January 1915 after receiving a shrapnel wound to his left leg. He was subsequently discharged from service on medical grounds in April 1915.

On the 4th October 1915 Jimmy's next youngest brother, Edward enlisted in the New Army, joining the 13th Royal Irish Rifles, a battalion which recruited mainly from County Down. He went to France the following year and fought within yards of his older brother at Thiepval on the 1st July 1916 where he won the Military medal for gallantry in the field. So, on the 26th February 1916 Sergeant Jimmy Scott paraded No.7 Platoon at Varennes for a work detail with his newly acquired diary in his pocket. It would be reasonable to assume that he had not decided on a use for the little book at that time. The book was pre-printed as a diary with a few lines apportioned to each day; no diary entries were ever recorded in it. Perhaps Jimmy Scott had learnt his lesson from the Boer War, no diaries to be kept or carried. Maybe he anticipated what was to come, for the 'B' Company No.7 Platoon Sergeant was not a New Army recruit, he was a seasoned player who had experienced the highs and lows of war, the victory alongside the humiliation of defeat. With a wife and five children back in Belfast it went without saying he wanted to survive but he knew that survival was not something that could be guaranteed in this modern industrialised war. For that reason he wrote nothing in the notebook, he kept it for a specific use. Within three weeks he had made the first entry.[8]

---

8 1916 Diary, James Scott, Scott Family Archive.

2

The List

W. LEITCH
21st March, Forceville

EARLY MARCH 1916 saw the 14th Royal Irish Rifles move into front line positions, holding them as a complete battalion rather than being chaperoned as they had been up to this time, alongside other units to gain front line experience.[1] The syllabus of further training which they had followed on landing in France had been completed and they were now regarded as a fully trained fighting unit, available for deployment along the 36th Divisional front. This inevitably meant that the unit would be moved to more active and dangerous sectors of the line. They had become part of the human build up for the anticipated 'big push' having previously assisted with the logistical infrastructure of the material build-up. The battalion moved to billets in the village of Mesnil situated on a ridge that ran parallel with the River Ancre, across the valley from Thiepval Ridge. The village by March 1916 had been practically destroyed by German artillery and was described by 14th R.I.R. 'A' Company signaller William McCormack in his diary as follows:[2]

> 'Mesnil, a village which is completely demolished by German Artillery, and not a single inhabitant in same. This place is 1 mile behind the firing line and shelled night and day. We slept in cellars here, as one never knew when the place would be shelled. We had one very heavy

---

1 National Archives, 14th R.I.R. War Diary, WO95/2511/1.
2 Diary of William McCormack, 'Keep Smiling', Nancy McCormack-Schaalje, Family collection.

bombardment here, when we had to 'stand to' and when morning came there was still less of our precious village to gaze upon.'

Movement during daylight was restricted for the men due to the frequency of the bombardments. From these billets in the reserve position the 14th R.I.R. rotated in and out of the front line at Hamel nearby. The main communication trench leading from the ruined village to the front line was known as Jacob's Ladder, a particularly dangerous trench that zig-zagged downhill from the ridge and presented an exposed target for enemy attention before it levelled and branched out towards a small burial ground then proceeded on and fed into to the trench system at Hamel village and the front line. In a matter of days the burial ground at the end of Jacob's Ladder began to be put to use as war began to take a toll on the young soldiers. On the afternoon of Wednesday the 15th March 1916 the Y.C.V.'s, having spent a period of five days in the front line positions at Hamel, were looking forward to being relieved in the line. The relief was to be carried out by the 11th Royal Inniskilling Fusiliers and was planned to commence at 4pm and be completed by 9.30pm. Preparing for the relief the Y.C.V.'s 'C' Company were in the reserve line of trenches, just behind and running parallel to the front trench. As the men set about preparing to leave the trenches their first experience of being on the receiving end of a new German weapon took them by surprise. Corporal Samuel Harrison described the event:[3]

'One of the German weapons was their deadly 'minewerfer' a sort of aerial torpedo. They are very costly I believe, and they can be seen as they travel through the air if a sharp lookout is kept. Unfortunately the first one wasn't seen and this dropped beside a young sergeant of ours, in a reserve trench, killing him instantly and wounding two or three others. A fearful explosion, followed by a

3 Diary of S. Harrison, R.U.R. Museum.

cloud of salmon coloured smoke, with bricks, sticks and everything in the vicinity going up in the air convinced us that some new atrocity was being perpetrated upon us. However, the next one was spotted in its flight and then we knew. About twelve in all came over.'

The young Sergeant mentioned was Charles (Carl) Penman of 5 Craigs Terrace in Belfast. His colleagues immediately attempted to recover his body but were forced to abandon the attempt and take cover as the remaining shells in the bombardment fell around them. This first casualty stunned the battalion. A number of diarists recorded the incident and word made its way back to family and friends in Belfast. A service of remembrance was held in his honour at the Shankill Road Mission hall on the evening of the 26th March, an account of which was published in the *Belfast News Letter* the following day:[4]

'The Late Sergeant Carl Penman.

Last evening a special interest attached to the service in connection with Shankill Road Mission owing to the announcement that a memorial service would be held in connection with the death of this gallant young soldier. Sergeant Carl Penman had been associated with the mission from his early boyhood. The platform last night was adorned with palms and flowers, and there was an overflowing and sympathetic congregation. The Rev. Dr. Montgomery delivered an address based on the words of St. Paul regarding David: 'He served his own congregation by the will of God'. Towards the close he said there was one thought present in the minds of nearly all those present that evening. A beautiful young life had been given up for King and country and for the great principles that lay behind this present dreadful war – principles for which good and brave men had contended throughout the world's history. Young Carl Penman endeared himself

---

4 *Belfast News Letter*, 'The Late Sergeant Carl Penman' 26th March 1916.

to all who knew him by his kindly, genial manner, his winsome disposition, his manly quality and his true Christian character. He set a noble example to the youths and young men of that congregation and in that district... Captain Hume and Lieutenants Sands and Gilmore were on the platform, with the 36th Company of the Boy's Brigade, to which the deceased sergeant belonged.'

Fellow 'C' Company colleague George Mullin noted Sergeant Penman's passing with a simple and sober empathy by writing: 'I feel sorry for his mother, as she is a widow.'[5]

So the battalion began to take casualties and suffer fatalities. Up to this point many of the young men had viewed their entry into the war as a big adventure; the reality however had begun to strike home. Following the death of Sergeant Penman the men returned to their underground cellar billets in the reserve positions beneath the ruined village of Hamel.

The geological make-up of that part of the Somme area played a part in determining the nature of injuries. The ground was made up of predominately flint and chalk presenting a relatively hard surface. Trench digging was difficult although once constructed, underground dug-outs proved resilient to artillery bombardments as the high explosive shells could not penetrate the ground, more often they exploded on impact with the hard surface. There was a deadly disadvantage to this effect. A shell bursting on the surface of the ground showered the area with shards of shrapnel, fragments of the shell case itself and also small metal balls packed into the high explosive that made up the internal structure of the shell. Anyone caught in the open and above ground in the vicinity of an artillery shell explosion risked death or serious injury from the metal that emanated from the site of the explosion and filled the air. Rifleman John Kennedy Hope MM described the ground in his memoirs:[6]

5 Diary of G Mullin, R.U.R. Museum.
6 Diary of J.K. Hope R.U.R. Museum.

'We hold the sector north of Hamel village. The trenches are in good order pure white chalk walls – the country all around is white chalk about 2 feet below a gravel surface and a most peculiar place. One would imagine it is the Sussex Downs. These are strong trenches with one terrible disadvantage. A shell bursts over the chalk – it doesn't sink – it spreads to kill – all of it. Not so in soft earth where the shell goes in and the metal mixes with the clay.'

On Sunday the 19th March 1916 the men of 'B' Company were in the reserve area trenches at Mesnil. The battalion was catching up with what was termed 'internal economy', repairing damaged trenches, cleaning equipment and weapons and ensuring supplies of food and ammunition were carried forward if required. Orders had just been received that they were to take over the front line again the next day, relieving the 11th Royal Inniskilling Fusiliers. That afternoon their positions came under German bombardment. As a result of the bombardment one man, twenty year old Rifleman William Fennel Leitch found himself caught in open ground and he was struck and severely wounded by shrapnel. William was attended to by battalion medics and was eventually evacuated to the casualty clearing station at Forceville, a village roughly four miles away beyond the Mesnil Ridge and safe from artillery strikes. William Leitch succumbed to his injuries and died at Forceville two days later on the 21st March 1916. He had lived at 5 Matilda Street in Belfast, the youngest son of John and Mary Leitch. William had worked at the pharmaceutical company, Thomas McMullan & Co, in Victoria Street in Belfast. This company would later be known as Sangers, Northern Ireland Limited and is still trading today. His family entered an 'In Memoriam' message in the *Belfast Evening Telegraph* three weeks later which, although simple in content, relayed the enormous grief felt by his family and touched on the added burden of having a son buried in a field far away which they would, in all reality, probably never be able to visit. Today we are acutely aware of the need for the bereaved to obtain closure; often this can be the act of burial and the marking of a grave as a place where loved ones can visit, spend time and pay their respects. There was very little by way of closure for those families bereaved of their young men during the Great War. The pain being even more unbearable for those who received a report of their loved ones being listed as 'missing' and whose lives would be thrown into a purgatory of having to constantly scour the pages of the local newspapers for scraps of information for years to come.

> 'Some day, some time our eyes shall see
> The face we loved so well;
> Some day our hands will clasp in his
> And never say farewell.
> Dear Willie, his memory never shall fade
> Nor his love till our hearts cease to beat;
> Though his mortal remains in the grave they have laid,
> Joy of joys in his presence we will meet.
> Sleeping somewhere in France.'

Between the time William Leitch was injured and his passing away at Forceville, Rifleman Samuel John Lewis, no 2915 was hit by machine gun fire and died of his wounds the following day.[7] He was laid to rest alongside William at Forceville on the 22nd March 1916. The funeral service was conducted by the Military Chaplain at that time, Captain Reverend Andrew Gibson, previously the Presbyterian Minister at Hill Street Presbyterian Church in Lurgan, County Armagh. Rifleman Lewis was 18 years and 10 months old at the time of his death and was the eldest son of Samuel and Mary Lewis of 28 Wimbledon Street in Belfast. He had worked in the General Post Office before enlisting and was involved with the Young Citizen Volunteers before the war. Samuel was not one of

---

7 14th R.I.R. Battalion Casualty Record, R.U.R. Museum.

Jimmy Scott's company, being a signaller with 'C' Company, 12 Platoon. The Reverend Gibson wrote to the family:[8]

> 'Your boy was buried in a little cemetery near the field hospital, where he rests with those who have made similar sacrifices in these tragic days. I conducted the funeral service. I was speaking to him before the end, and he realised that he was going to die, and met his death resignedly. This is a sore trial, but I pray that God will strengthen you to meet and bear it in the spirit of trust and he will comfort you in your day of shadow and sorrow.'

On Tuesday the 21st March 1916 Sergeant Jimmy Scott removed the little book that he had kept untouched from his pocket and prepared to make the first entry, the time had come for him to put the book to the use that he had intended. For the first time in fifteen years he had lost a member of his section in combat, killed in action. Whether it was the experience of dealing with colleagues killed in battle in South Africa or perhaps a new sense of responsibility that came with his Sergeant rank or just a feeling that it was the right thing to do; maybe he had an idea that in the chaos of war such simple details would be invaluable later on to family or loved ones. Whatever his train of thought the note was made using the little pencil attached to the book, 'W Leitch 24th March, (Forceville)'. Jimmy Scott had recorded the first member of 'B' Company to be killed and the name of the cemetery where he was buried.

The routine of occupying the front line trenches and providing working parties to assist the Royal Engineers between Hamel and Mesnil continued on into April 1916. On the 2nd April the battalion once again took up positions in the trench systems at Hamel. By this time the front line trenches were being bombed with German trench mortars more frequently and on a daily basis. A build up of enemy

---

8 *Belfast News Letter*, 6th May 1916.

activity continued until on Thursday 6th April the battalion was ordered to stand to at 7.00p.m. Shortly after, at around 9.00p.m. a bombardment commenced, lasting for almost two hours. Those occupying the front line trench quickly realised that the German artillery had found the range of their positions. As the trench began to be pulverised they were forced to leave it and lie in the open forward of their own barbed wire lines in 'no man's land' in an attempt to escape the deadly destruction. The order was given to open fire, as it was perceived that an enemy raid was about to take place. The men of the 14th Royal Irish maintained a steady rapid rate of rifle fire although no enemy could be seen by the men in the trenches, reports received later from aerial observers would maintain that a disaster was averted. The wall of fire put down by the battalion had prevented the German soldiers from carrying out the raid on the Y.C.V. lines. The battalion to the left of them, part of the 29th Division were not so lucky. The German raid broke their line and a large number of prisoners were taken. The activity tailed off at around 11.30pm. On taking stock and tidying up after the action it was apparent that more casualties had been taken. Jimmy Scott added to his list the name:

G DORRITY
6th April (Hamel)

Rifleman George Dorrity, 16443, was attached to 'B' Company, Jimmy's company. He was 21 years of age. On enlisting, he had lived at 37 Pretoria Street in Belfast's Stranmillis area having originally come from Ballylesson just a few miles south of the city. George was buried at Hamel cemetery. In death he was not alone. He was laid to rest along with four of his comrades also killed that night. Rifleman George Foster of 12 platoon, Sergeant William Stephenson, who had been part of Jimmy Scott's winning tug of war team the previous year, being originally a member of 'B' company, transferring to 'D' company on the 27th November 1915. Rifleman Randolph Campbell from the King's Road in Belfast also lost his life. A second rifleman with the surname Campbell, Alex Campbell from Nore Street in Belfast died the following day from his wounds and was also buried at Forceville Cemetery close to the casualty clearing station.

The remainder of April 1916 passed without any further additions to the list. On the last day of the month Jimmy Scott and 'B' Company took up new positions on the far side of the Ancre River opposite Hamel. The battalion entered Thiepval Wood. The men looked upon Thiepval Wood as just another trench position to adapt to and become familiar with. The name meant nothing out of the ordinary to them as they were not to know that within weeks and for years to come the word Thiepval would become synonymous with death, destruction and the grief of the population of Ulster. Indeed, to the contrary, the natural beauty of the wood itself and the nearby village of Authuile in that spring of 1916 had a positive impact on the men. Their new sector, from the leafy beauty of Thiepval Wood itself stretched back from the front lines towards the approach to the village where the ground falls away today as it did then to meet the wide and slowly flowing Ancre River which babbled by unhindered, severing the British and German lines. The steepness of the valley's side between Authuile and the river itself provided a natural defensive leeward slope, safe from artillery fire and the deadly stroke of the 'devil's paintbrush' as the German Maxim machine guns were known. With long established well constructed positions in Thiepval village itself and along the infamous Schwaben Redoubt, the German stronghold dug deep into the high ground overlooking Thiepval Wood. The German force held the height advantage, the wood and the steep slope towards the river offered a place of safety close to the front line. The weather was kind to the two armies, spring had arrived in all of her glory and amongst the steadily build-up of paraphernalia and expanding man–made earthworks, nature continued on its course. The men were in buoyant mood and on the face of it, pleased with their new working environment. On the 1st May Signaller McCormack took in his surroundings and recorded in his diary:[9]

'The good weather continues and as I was off duty until 2.30pm I had a fine bathe in the Ancre River. This river is in full view of the German lines, but small parties are very rarely interfered with and during my whole time here I only had to beat a hasty retreat once whilst bathing as Fritz started to splash us with a few whizz-bangs. The fresh smell of the woods, the scorching sun, birds singing and a sparkling river left nothing to be desired. So I returned feeling in A1 form. The trenches in this part of the line were fine, the nicest ever we were in. They were nice and wide and water taps were in the trenches! This to us was a treat, as we were never able to get a wash in the trenches before. In fact, after what we had been through in other parts of the line, such as Auchonvillers, where we were up to the waist in mud, we looked upon this spell as a sort of picnic.'

Thiepval Wood soon turned out to be far from a picnic. Before long Jimmy Scott put pencil to paper once more.

W. H. GRAINGER
3rd May, Authuille nr. Martinsart.

William Grainger was 21 years old and although not a member of 'B' company Jimmy had kept an eye out for him, noting his name and the cemetery where he was buried. The reason was that William Grainger lived just eight doors away from James and Jane Scott in Elm Street in Belfast. He had worked as a clerk and had known the Scott family well. William Grainger was killed following a bombardment that lasted for most of

---

9 Diary of William McCormack, 'Keep Smiling', Nancy McCormack-Schaalje, Family collection.

the morning of the 3rd May 1916. Ten others were wounded and two men were described as suffering from 'shell shock' by signaller McCormack.

William Grainger's death appears to have had the effect of changing Jimmy's thinking on the criteria for including names on his list. Initially it seemed that he had recorded the names of only those members of 'B' Company who were killed, William was attached to 'C' company. He was however a neighbour of Jimmy. His death perhaps reinforced Jim's sense of responsibility for the men he trained. In William's case he knew him as he grew from child to young adult and from his days as a member of the Young Citizen Volunteers prior to the outbreak of war. Had Jim been an influence in William making the decision to enlist? Had he been in admiration of the Boer War veteran as he made his way to and from work along Elm Street and the Donegall Pass in Belfast, walking with the unmistakable bearing and confidence of an army veteran? We cannot know the answer to these questions but Jimmy recorded the name in the little book. Any return home now to Elm Street would be a difficult experience; the Sergeant would have to face the Grainger family without their son.

Rifleman Grainger was later laid to rest in Authuile Cemetery alongside Lance Corporal William McLauchlan from Millford, County Armagh, killed the previous day during a separate mortar bombardment. Rifleman Arnold Hayden from Ashley Avenue off Belfast's Lisburn Road was one of those wounded in the attack that killed William Grainger. He succumbed to his wounds and passed away at the Casualty Clearing Station at Beauval on Thursday the 4th May 1916. The steady attrition continued with four more casualties for the Y.C.V. men, wounded by artillery fire as the German gunners ranged their guns on various parts of the Thiepval trench system. That night, and into the early hours of Friday the 5th the guns of the newly formed 109th Brigade

Machine Gun Company were active in the Thiepval sector. At around 4.30 am one of their teams had spotted an enemy sniper attempting to move into a firing point and a belt of 250 rounds was fired at his position. For the 14th Royal Irish Rifles the morning gave way to what was described in their War Diary as 'a perfect summer's day'. Orders had been received that the 32nd Division to their right (15th Lancashire Fusiliers) were to carry out a raid on the German positions opposite at about midnight. With regard to the raid the 14th R.I.R. were 'to make their own arrangements'[10]. The companies were warned to man the front line and keep low and to be ready for any emergency. In initially taking up their positions during the trench relief earlier that week a mistake had been made that meant their 'D' Company had filed into the trenches to the right of their sector and established their positions instead of the left which then became occupied by 'A' and 'B' Companies. This mistake was not corrected as by the time it was discovered the men had taken up their positions and settled into their trenches. Rather than cause disruption and further activity along the lines at a critical time it was decided to keep the positions as they were. By the time the night of the 5th May 1916 had passed it would be discovered that luck had dealt a devastating hand to the men of 'D' Company, allowing Jimmy Scott's 'B' Company something of a reprieve in the cruel game of war.

At the stroke of midnight a terrific artillery barrage was unleashed onto the German lines. The bombardment was directed across the planned point of entry of the Lancashire Fusiliers raiding party into the German trenches on a front of approximately 200 yards across. This point of entry was located opposite the left flank of the 32nd Division sector, bordering on the right of the sector held by the 14th Royal Irish Rifles. It was planned that the raiding party would not carry out their raid directly opposite their own lines in order that their

10 National Archives, 14th R.I.R. War Diary, WO95/2511/1.

retreat would be unhindered by any retaliation. At 00.33hrs on the 6th May 1916 the Lancashire Fusiliers' raiding party entered the German front line trenches, four 'snatch' teams quickly moving from dug-out to dug-out, man-handling prisoners out of their protection and bringing them out of the trench where the remnants of the party covered their return to the British lines. Two prisoners were taken almost immediately with a further three following within minutes. In total five prisoners were taken and a number of the dug-outs were bombed. A half hearted attempt was made to counter-attack the raiding party but this was repulsed using grenades. Nevertheless, along with their haul of prisoners the Lancashires had suffered casualties. The bodies of five of their party, killed during the raid, were carried back across no man's land to their own lines. As the raiders left the enemy lines the Germans began a retaliation, initially using trench mortars but then following up with a deadly artillery barrage onto the sector of trenches directly opposite the point of entry made on their positions by the raiding party, the sector held by the 14th Royal Irish Rifles. Almost immediately the battalion headquarters of the 14th Royal Irish Rifles was rocked by a large mortar explosion; night turned to day with the intensity of the retaliatory bombardment. The 'D' Company commander, Lieutenant Jerome Lennie Walker, ordered his company to 'stand to' at their posts anticipating a counter raid. The men of 'D' company turned out of their protective 'funk holes' and dug-outs and manned the fire step of their front line encouraged by their commander. Walker, throughout the bombardment, paced up and down behind his men shouting cheerful encouragement in anticipation of finally engaging his enemy, keeping his men ready at their posts. In the headquarters dug-out, named Gordon Castle, the situation was beginning to look increasingly serious to Captain Harper. Communication by telephone with 'D' company had been lost at an early stage of the bombardment, followed by loss of communication between the battalion and the 16th Lancashire Fusiliers on their right, the wires for the field telephones had been severed by exploding shells. Any communication now had to be made by runners, risking life to carry information to and from the companies in the line. This activity was severely hampered by German machine gun fire sweeping through the barrage along the British support and communication trenches.

At approximately 01.25hrs a runner, Rifleman Milligan from Roden Street in Belfast, managed to carry a message to Captain Harper at Gordon Castle having come through a wall of shellfire from 'D' company's line and reported that the company had suffered 10 casualties. The artillery fire had become so intense that the exploding shells began to bring down trees in the wood which crashed to the ground across the trenches, further hampering communications. Eventually, with the bombardment at its peak, a trench protecting a platoon of 'D' Company collapsed, burying alive the men in it. At 02.30hrs Lieutenant Walker regained communications with his headquarters after a telephone wire had been re-laid by a signaller. He reported 'a number of his men had been buried by a trench coming in on them'. The full extent of the carnage inflicted now became apparent. A squad of men led by the pioneer Sergeant, Tom Murphy, began frantically digging to attempt to rescue their colleagues, exposing themselves to heavy machine gun and shell fire as they worked. The Lewis Gun teams, brought together by Lance Corporal Steele, began laying down covering fire as the remainder of the battalion not engaged in holding the line began a frantic rescue operation to excavate the collapsed trench. At around this time a shrapnel shell exploded directly above Lieutenant Walker decapitating him and killing Rifleman Edward Adams who was beside him at the time. Chaos reigned right along the sector. At Hammerhead Sap, a part of the front line trench system close to the now ruined Thiepval Chateau, a similar story was unfolding. The sap had been used to site one of the 109th Brigade Machine Gun Company's Vickers heavy machine guns. During the bombardment the gun and team were also buried alive along with seven or eight men of the 16th Lancashire Fusiliers. One of the gunners, Private Thomas Bottoms who was from Durham and had previously served with the Inniskilling Fusiliers, somehow managed to extricate himself from the debris and then, under heavy fire, used his own entrenching tool to dig out the remainder of the buried men, saving their lives. The gun itself was also recovered the next morning, still intact. Thomas was later awarded the Military Medal for his actions that night. He was killed on the 1st July 1916. His name appears on the Thiepval Memorial to the Missing.

By 03.00hrs on the morning of the 6th May 1916 the barrage died down and a period of relative quiet returned to Thiepval Wood. The men of the 14th Royal Irish Rifles 'stood to' as dawn broke and the roll was called. There were many who did not answer. 'A' Company Scout, Rifleman James McRoberts, described the period of calm following the bombardment:[11]

> 'Before dawn the order came "Stand to, Germans over the parapet." We stood to and a large party of Germans was seen gathering up their casualties, men who had evidently been caught out on one of their working parties. The order "No firing" was passed and they were allowed to finish their work in peace.'

For what was described as a 'successful' raid the Lancashires had paid a high price. The Irishman leading the raid, Captain Robert John Smith, was killed as was his 20 year old 2nd Lieutenant, John Ramsay Younger from Manchester along with Sergeant Brooks and Privates Wall and Leeming from Salford. Five others were wounded. In addition to the 15th

---

11 *Young Citizen Old Soldier*, Diary of James McRoberts edited by David Truesdale, Helion and Company 2012.

Lancashires' casualties their 16th battalion on the front line lost one man with fourteen wounded. The 2nd Royal Inniskilling Fusiliers manning the sector to the right of the 16th Lancashires lost two men with another fourteen wounded. The 14th Royal Irish Rifles suffered dearly. In addition to the loss of Lieutenant Walker, twelve men were killed and a total of twenty-nine were wounded, two later dying of their wounds. In total, the casualties along the Thiepval sector on the morning of the 6th May 1916 numbered three officers and eighteen men killed with sixty-two wounded. That morning the men of the 14th Royal Irish Rifles along with the Lancashire Fusiliers cleared up the debris in their trenches and buried their dead at the little cemetery at Authuile. The Young Citizens, after then being relieved in the line by the 9th Inniskilling Fusiliers, marched to their hutted billets beside Martinsart. There they spent Sunday the 7th May cleaning equipment and catching up with much needed sleep; for the moment their spell at the front line was over and they would leave the Thiepval area the next day. For those that remained holding the line the nightmare continued.

It had been known to the men of the Y.C.V. that the 9th Inniskilling Fusiliers had planned to carry out a raid on the German lines from the Thiepval sector. Indeed the raiding party, selected and led by second in command of the battalion, Major Warren John Richard Peacocke, answerable to Colonel Ambrose Ricardo, had been training specifically for the operation for eight days prior to the raid at the training grounds at Clairfaye where training trenches replicating the German lines opposite Thiepval had been constructed. This, the first raid to be carried out by the 36th (Ulster) Division, was planned to take place on the night of the 7th May 1916. With the honour of the Division and that of the 9th Inniskilling Fusiliers at stake, Major Peacocke planned the raid with meticulous attention to detail. The adage often considered by those burdened with the task of trying to account for every possibility in such endeavours was unfortunately on this occasion to ring true in that no plan, however well conceived, survives first contact with the enemy.

At 20.30hrs on the night of the 7th May the first party of men involved in the raid made their way from the British front line into no man's land.[12] The party, led by 2nd Lieutenant Leonard Stevenson and made up of a Sergeant and five men established a temporary headquarters for the raid in the Sunken Road, the name given to the Thiepval – Hamel Road which ran in front of Thiepval Wood. Here they monitored the German lines and the situation in no man's land until 22.45hrs when they were joined by a second party of three men led by Captain Weir. Captain Weir's team then began to lay tape along the proposed route to the enemy lines while they were covered by Lieutenant Stevenson's party. Meanwhile, in the battalion reserve trenches, the main party paraded and were inspected by Lieutenant Furness. He made a final check of their equipment and ensured that the party had removed all identifying badges and numerals, were not in possession of any documents or letters and had blackened their faces. The various parties of men then left the British front lines from 23.00hrs in eight groups, separated by two minute intervals, to re-group in the Sunken Road. They had no sooner left the British line when the German artillery commenced an intense bombardment on the trenches of the 1st Dorsetshire Regiment who had taken over the sector immediately to the right of the Inniskillings. This bombardment continued for approximately twenty minutes and then switched to bombard the Inniskilling's own line and support trenches steadily increasing in intensity. By this time all of the members of the raiding party were out in no man's land, making their way towards the Sunken Road. At 23.40hrs the final party arrived in Sunken Road having laid

12 National Archives, 9th Royal Inniskilling Fusiliers War Diary, WO95/2510/603

a telephone wire behind them. Major Peacocke then spoke to Colonel Ricardo in the headquarters dug-out in Thiepval Wood. Up to this point Colonel Ricardo had held the fire of the British artillery as the British guns were already trained on the barrage lines to be used to support the raid. It was decided to continue with the raid in spite of the German bombardment. In any case, there could now be no safe return for the raiding party; they had 'shot their bolt' and had to follow through with the proposed raid.

At 23.45hrs the British bombardment began in support of the raid as planned, laying down fire on the German front lines and wire. The raiders now had no choice but to remain low in no man's land, taking advantage of whatever cover they could find between two artillery bombardments until at 00.10hrs on the 8 May the British bombardment lifted onto the German support trenches, behind the trenches to be raided, in order to prevent any counter attack on the raiding party. At this point 2nd Lieutenant Stevenson and his team, who had now been between the lines for almost four hours, quickly moved forward to check the state of the German wire ahead of deploying a Bangalore torpedo explosive device which it was planned to use to clear the wire. Stevenson's quick reconnaissance and accurate assessment of the state of the enemy wire saved valuable minutes as he discovered that the explosive was not necessary; the artillery had effectively cut a swathe through the wire. The Inniskillings then charged forward from the Sunken Road, following the tape previously laid by Captain Weir and entered the German trenches in their various parties as they had rehearsed time and time again at Clairfaye over the previous week. One team along with Major Peacocke remained in the Sunken Road to maintain communications with Headquarters at Gordon Castle and cover their extraction. The remaining raiding parties entered the trenches and bombed a number of dug-outs. Unfortunately the German defenders, for reasons that were soon to become obvious, were found to be on the alert and stiff resistance was met. Lance Sergeant William Barker, on entering the trenches, became immediately aware that the enemy were beginning to come up out from their dug-outs. He quickly ran to the dug-out entrance and shot the first enemy troops as they started to emerge, stopping any further troops from making it back into the trench. No prisoners could be taken as it proved impossible to extricate the German defenders from their dug-outs. After spending a total of eleven minutes fighting in the enemy trenches the raiding party withdrew back through the gap in the wire and re-grouped in the Sunken Road. They had suffered relatively few casualties during the actual raid. Lance Corporal Gilbert McIntrye was killed attempting to block the trench system being raided against counter attack when his party were heavily bombed; his team leader, Sergeant Gibson and another man were injured. Sergeant Barker managed to recover Gilbert McIntyre's body under fire and eventually bring him back to the Sunken Road. The night was far from over.

By a remarkable coincidence, as the 9th Inniskilling Fusiliers were entering the German trenches a raiding party, consisting of around one hundred men of the German 99th Reserve Infantry Regiment (99th R.I.R.) began raiding the sector immediately to the right of that held by the 36th Division, held now by the 32nd Divisions' 1st Dorsetshire Regiment, about 250 yards further along the British lines. The reason for the earlier bombardment now became clear. The German raid was in retaliation for that carried out on the night of the 6th May by the 15th Lancashire Fusiliers, the bombardment being a prelude to the raid. The men of the 99th R.I.R. entered the Dorsetshire trenches at three points between Hammerhead Sap and a trench known as Foxbar Street opposite Oblong Wood. An intense, vicious battle now began in the British front line trenches with the German gunners employing a similar technique to their enemy of bombarding the support and reserve trenches behind in order to isolate the sector being raided. The Dorsetshire Regiment suffered heavy casualties as brutal hand-to-hand fighting forced those not already injured in the barrage out of the front line trenches; a large number of prisoners were taken including men from the 109th Brigade Machine Gun Company who were manning the machine gun at Hammerhead Sap. An immediate request was made from the 32nd division to their neighbouring 36th division for assistance to help repel the raiders from their lines. Straight away, half a company, between 80 and 90 men from the 10th Royal Inniskilling Fusiliers, the 'Derrys,' resting in reserve at Authuile, made their way at speed to the Dorsetshire sector. Two machine gun teams from the 109th company were also pushed forward into the area along with the brigade bombing section; the reinforcements had first to make their way through the deadly covering artillery barrage engulfing Thiepval Wood.

At about this time the 9th Inniskillings raiding party was effectively stranded in Sunken Road, unable to return to their lines due to the same sustained barrage covering the German raid. They remained exposed there for one and a half hours, continually taking casualties to shrapnel from the artillery shells falling around them. In total twenty-two men were wounded and one man, Lance Corporal John Fox, was lost completely after literally being blown away by the direct hit from an artillery shell. Despite frantic searching, no trace could be found of him. The raiding party eventually made it back to their own lines at about 02.45hrs. They brought all of their wounded back. Sergeant William Barker carried the body of his comrade Lance Corporal Gilbert McIntyre, of Bootle Street in Belfast, from where he fell in the German lines back to the Sunken Road where he was forced to lie with him for that terrifying hour and a half until the bombardment eased. He was then finally able to return, carrying his body across no man's land to the lines held by his own battalion.

The German raiding party had meanwhile been finally forced out of the British lines by the counter attack made by the Derrys. In the violent struggle one German officer was killed and a second taken prisoner. There had however been many prisoners taken from the 1st Dorsetshire Regiment. Among them another Ulsterman, 27 year old Corporal William Millar from Park Street, Coleraine, County Londonderry. Corporal Millar had previously served with the Derrys as a Private and had transferred to the 109th Brigade Machine Gun Company where he had been promoted to Corporal. On the night of the 7th May he was the non-commissioned officer in charge of the Vickers gun team at Hammerhead Sap. As a result of the German surprise raid he found himself taken prisoner and led out through his own wire at the point of a German bayonet. We cannot know now exactly what was going through his mind, but his subsequent actions can give us more than a slight idea of how he felt. Whatever his motivation, William Millar was not going to simply walk into the hands of his enemy, he decided to fight what was to be his final battle. Just as William cleared the final stretch of his own wire he, along with a young Dorsetshire officer 19 year old 2nd Lieutenant Vere Talbot Bayly from Bath, decided to take on their captors. Bayly and Millar turned on the Germans escorting them and a vicious hand to hand fight ensued. In the confusion that followed many of the Dorsetshire prisoners grasped the opportunity and managed to dodge their German captors and make good their escape back to their own trenches. Corporal Millar and Lieutenant Bayly, unarmed, were eventually overpowered and bayoneted by the German raiders, their bodies left in no man's land to be recovered later and brought back to their own line. Captain Maconachie of the Machine Gun Company wrote a letter to William's widow. Part of this letter was printed in the 13 May 1916 edition of the *Belfast News Letter* and read as follows:[13]

---

13 *Belfast News Letter*, Ulster and The War, 'Died Fighting Desperately', 13th May 1916.

'After a terrible bombardment on the 7th inst. the Germans broke into the British lines and attempted to take Corporal Miller prisoner. Although greatly out numbered he showed magnificent courage and lost his life while fighting desperately.'

The incident was also recorded in the 109th Infantry Brigade War Diary by Lieutenant Kenneth Moore who included in his entry:[14]

'A large number of the enemy entered our trenches at Queen's Cross Street, Hammerhead Sap and for about 20 yards to the right of that sap. It is believed that an officer of the Dorsets and an N.C.O. put up a fight when being taken over our wire, as they were found there dead, with several bayonet wounds.'

As the situation along the front at Thiepval once again returned to relative calm the Derrys continued to hold the Dorsetshire's sector of the line until they could eventually replace the men lost during the raid from their reserves. The roll call and burial parties commenced with the little cemetery at Authuile becoming a hive of grim activity. The 9th Inniskillings had lost a total of eighteen men killed with eighty-four wounded. Seven of these men died later from their wounds. The 1st Dorsetshires had suffered thirteen men killed, twenty-nine wounded and twenty-four were 'missing', having been taken prisoner. Within the space of just over forty-eight hours, between midnight on the 5th May and the early morning of the 8th May 1916, the casualties along the two hundred and fifty yard front at Thiepval Wood amounted to over two hundred and twenty men killed or wounded with twenty-four 'missing' or taken prisoner. Between them, the 32nd and 36th Divisions fronting on the Thiepval sector had in total, taken only six German prisoners to show for their efforts.

If the results of the operations over the three days

14 National Archives, War Diaries, 36 Div 109 Infantry Brigade, WO95/2507/2

that this war was different from that which he had previously experienced. In the short time that he had spent at the front he and his men had endured artillery bombardments the like of which he had never endured in four years of fighting in South Africa. He was a Sergeant in charge of a platoon of Ulstermen, he had new responsibilities and fears. These were men whom he had known before the war. In the most part he knew their families, fathers, mothers, wives and brothers. He knew where and how they had lived and he had witnessed how they had died. Regardless now of company or platoon, or of any petty rivalries or competition fostered during training and on the move up to the line, Jimmy now stood before his brothers. He could simply have done nothing and walked on his way past the cemetery to Blackhorse Bridge, crossed the Ancre and continued on to his billet at Martinsart. He decided to remove the little pencil from where it had been held securely through the night's bombardment and in a shaky hand he began to write:

'Authulle (nr. Martinsart)
Killed night of the 5th April'

At this point he incorrectly wrote 'April' instead of 'May' and corrected his mistake by writing one word on top of the other, perhaps an indication of where his mind was at that time. He continued the entry as follows:

'Lt. Walker
Pte Beattie
McBratney
Martin
Adams
Sloane
McKeown
L/Cpl Lowe
Pte Tollerton
Pte Walker.'

JEROME LENNIE WALKER

Jerome Lennie Walker was the 2nd Lieutenant in charge
of number 13 platoon, 'D' Company on the night of the
5th May 1916. He had obtained his commission in early
January 1915 and trained with the 14th Royal Irish Rifles
at Randalstown in County Antrim and Seaford in England
before deploying with them to France. Before the outbreak
of the war Jerome lived at 31 Boulevard Van Der Peereboome
in Kortrijk (Courtrai) in Belgium. This was an affluent area
of Courtrai close to the railway station and not far from the
family's flax business offices at Ouai De Republique. The
family business, 'Reilly and Walker' had initially been based
in Belfast. Due to a slump in the flax trade at the turn of the
century Jerome's father, Franklyn Manderson Walker, had set
up trading offices in both Rotterdam in Holland and Ghent
in Belgium, leading him to eventually move from his home
at Whitehouse near Larne in County Antrim to manage the
business and set up a new home in Courtrai in July 1904.
Jerome, in 1905, returned to Belfast where he attended school
at Campbell College prior to taking up employment in the
family business back in Courtrai.

On the 4th August 1914, the German Army entered
Belgium intending to pass through to carry out a swift
sweeping attack on France. This attack was designed to defeat
the French quickly by surprise and then leave the German
army ready to face her ally, Russia, whom it was anticipated
would take time to mobilise in defence and subsequently also
be easily defeated. At 8.30am the German army crossed into
neutral Belgium, intent on sweeping quickly through the
country and attacking France from its northern border. By
midnight that night Great Britain was at war with Germany
and had committed to defend France and Belgium. In the
meantime the Belgians, rather than allow the German army
unhindered passage, dug in and put up a fierce resistance
against the German forces, delaying their advance. Living

in Courtrai, Jerome and his family anxiously watched the progress of the German army. After the first week of hostilities Jerome's father, Franklyn Manderson Walker, made the decision to leave the family home and move to his business premises at 14 Pelikaanstraat in Rotterdam. Jerome remained at Courtrai and volunteered with the Red Cross Society. On the 18th October 1914 British troops entered the Belgian town of Roeselare ahead of the German army. Jerome watched the event after travelling there in a motor car owned by his family. At some point during the day he was informed that the German army had massed at Courtrai itself; Jerome's return route to Courtrai had therefore been cut off. He made his way to Ypres, effectively a refugee.

The German forces soon directed their advance towards Ypres, forcing many of the town's residents to flee. In Ypres Jerome became aware of the plight of the patients of the town's Hospital of Sacre-Cour, known as the Asylum. By the first week in November many of the hospital officials had fled and the patients were left in the care of the residential caretaker, Gustaaf Delahaye. As German artillery shells began to land dangerously close to the hospital building arrangements were made to evacuate the patients, a process which eventually took eleven days in total, between the 10th and 21st November 1914. Jerome volunteered to help and with his motor car assisted in the evacuation, moving many patients to safety in Paris. Jerome then found himself trapped in Ypres and resorted to sheltering in a cellar for the duration of what was the First Battle of Ypres before eventually making his way to the English Channel and then back to Belfast via London. On his return to Belfast Jerome stayed at 7 Ashville, Skegoneill Avenue. This was the home of Isabella Gladys MacDonald. The extent of his relationship with her is not known. There are indications that she may have been a nurse and perhaps shared his adventure in Belgium as records exist of a nurse sharing the same name and age; it cannot be confirmed, however, that this was the same person.

What is certain is that Jerome Walker was determined to return to Belgium in an attempt to take back his home and family business. With Europe now well in the grip of a terrible war, the only option open to him was to fight. He applied for a commission in the Royal Irish Rifles on his return to Belfast on the 17th December 1914. He was appointed 2nd Lieutenant with the 14th Battalion on the 3rd January 1915. He trained with the battalion at Finner and Randalsown camps, taking charge of no. 13 platoon, part of 'D' Company. Lieutenant Jerome Lennie Walker was the first member of the Young Citizen Volunteers to have experienced being under enemy fire in Belgium, as a civilian. He was also the first officer to be killed in action while serving with the battalion on the front line in France. He never did make it back to Belgium. Following his death his medals, issued in 1922, were bequeathed to Isabella MacDonald. On the 9th May 1916 Jerome's father, Franklyn Manderson Walker received a telegram from his business address in Rotterdam sent to temporary accommodation in Helen's Bay near Crawfordsburn in County Down informing him of the death of his son. He penned the following reply to The Secretary of The War Office:[17]

'Sir, I have received the following wire from Rotterdam: This telegram received. Deeply regret to inform you that 2/Lt J L Walker Irish Rifles was killed in action 5th May. Lord Kitchener expresses his sympathy. Secretary War Office.' Lieut. Walker was my only son. I hear he died doing his duty in the trenches. I have been in Rotterdam all winter and only recently returned. If he left anything behind I would be pleased to have them sent to this address not for their value but as souvenirs. Our residence was in Courtrai, my family left there first week of the war and we left everything behind and the Germans seized all.

17 National Archives, Officer's File, 2Lt. J.L. Walker WO339/16748

They've been occupying our house since. Thanking you in anticipation.
I remain, Sir
your obedient servant.
F M Walker'

Franklyn Walker returned to Courtrai after the war in October 1920. He took a room at the Terminus Public House at Marketplace 31 in Courtrai. He died while residing at that same address in October 1924.

ALBERT BEATTIE

Rifleman Albert Beattie no. 14/17242 was a bugler in 'C' Company of the 14th Royal Irish Rifles. He originally came from 42 Clifton Street in Belfast, living there with his father David Alexander, mother Jane, three sisters Rebecca, Mabel and Daisy and his brother, David. His father was a tobacconist in Belfast at the time of the 1901 census. In the years before the outbreak of the war Albert found himself tragically orphaned and living under the care of the Balmoral Industrial School at Ballygomartin in Belfast. The industrial schools at that time had been established to care for destitute or orphaned children and were also used to detain children who had become involved in petty crime. Albert, in spite of the distressing circumstances under which he found himself living and under the more direct care of the school secretary, Mr. James Bell, developed an interest in music and learnt to play the baritone horn. He became a member of the Balmoral Industrial School brass band. On leaving the industrial school he became involved with the Independent Order of Rechabites Friendly Society (I.O.R.). This total abstinence charitable organisation was founded in Belfast in 1846 with the objective of providing relief to its members in sickness and to provide assistance to members' widows and orphans. It is highly likely that Albert and his brothers and sisters came under the care of this organisation after they were orphaned.

The I.O.R. held their meetings in halls and homes at various locations across Belfast and further afield in Banbridge, Newry and Londonderry. They referred to their meeting rooms as 'Tents', a term which reflected on the biblical roots of the organisation. Albert was a member of 'The Rescue' Tent whose members met at the Magdalene Schoolroom in Great Victoria Street in Belfast. Albert Beattie also played in the I.O.R. Rescue Tent band. At the outbreak of war Albert Beattie enlisted with the 14th Battalion. He gave the address of his sister, living at 93 Emerson Street in Belfast, as his next of kin. During training and following his deployment to France in October 1915 Albert struck up a friendship with a signaller in 'A' Company called William McCormack. William, in his role as signaller, could move between companies in the battalion and had more of a free rein across the battalion than an ordinary Rifleman. William McCormack survived the war and kept a record in the form of a diary. In it he describes his feelings on the loss of his best friend, Albert Beattie:[18]

> 'Our right company got a fearful battering, and one platoon was buried alive. Besides a frightful number of dead, wounded and missing. One officer having his head blown clean off, also a chum of my own – Albert Beattie. The straffe lasted from 12 midnight until 1.30am. Needless to say we were all glad when it was all over, as our right company suffered heavily. And when dawn did appear with the fresh smell of the woods, and the birds chirping cheerfully – Oh, the irony of it. Other mornings I enjoyed it immensely, but this particular morning I felt very sad when I thought of Albert Beattie and all my other fallen comrades. To think that yesterday morning they also enjoyed the scenery and the birds. And today the birds sing on, quite unconscious of what has taken place.

18 Diary of William McCormack, 'Keep Smiling', Nancy McCormack-Schaalje, Family Collection

Oh! The irony of war on a lovely spring morn. Some way or other the birds seem like discord to me and the air is poisonous, but enough. Gods' will be done'.

Before his death Albert Beattie had written a will into the page of his soldier's paybook, army book No. 64, which was printed with a page allocated for the purpose. Details of a will entered in the book in this way during a soldier's active service were deemed to be legally binding in the event of the soldier being killed in action. In the case of a rank and file soldier obtaining a commission, details of a will made in this way would still be regarded as legally binding should he be killed in action later as an officer. The date of the will is not known but the entry in Albert's book records the following:[19]

> 'In the event of my death, which I hope will be an honourable one on the field of battle I appoint my sisters Mabel Gibson and Miss D Beattie to my shares of my fathers will, also the remainder of my property. Pte A Beattie 14 (S) R.I.Rifles'

Albert Beattie was 24 years old at the time of his death.

JOHN HENRY McBRATNEY

Rifleman McBratney originally came from Comber Bridge, Ballynahinch in County Down. On joining the 14th Royal Irish Rifles in September 1914 he was attached to 'D' Company and was under the command of Lieutenant Walker on the night of the 5th May 1916. As the war progressed his family moved to Comber in County Down and lived there at 28 Brownlow Street. John's brother, Samuel served with the Royal Engineers. He was a joiner and wheelwright by trade and survived the war, eventually taking up a position in the Civil Service in 1924. The family connections with the war did not end there as John's uncle, James Healey also served the colours and was killed in action on the 27th April 1916, just over a week before John's death while serving with with

---

19 National Archives of Ireland, Soldier's Wills, NAI/2002/119, E/199591/1

the 2nd Battalion of the Royal Munster Fusiliers. Four years after his death the pain felt by his family was still apparent and could be seen by all who read the 'In Memoriam' columns of the *Belfast Evening Telegraph* on the anniversary of his death in May 1920 which stated:[20]

> 'McBRATNEY – In memory of Private J H McBratney, Y.C.V., killed on the 6th May 1916; also my brother, Private J Healey, Munster Fusiliers, killed on the 27th April 1916. Four years ago today, our hearts still sore; As time goes on we miss them more. Ever remembered by his loving mother, father, sisters and brother, 28 Brownlow Street, Comber'

John Henry McBratney was 24 years old at the time of his death. He is remembered on the Comber town war memorial.

THOMAS MARTIN

Thomas Martin came from the Springfield Road in Belfast. Before the war he worked in his father's grocery shop at number 314 Springfield Road, where the family also lived. Thomas joined the 14th Royal Irish Rifles in September 1914 and trained with the battalion at Finner, Randalstown and Seaford before embarking for France on the 5th October 1915. On his arrival in France Thomas was immediately selected to be temporarily attached to No. 4 Company Army Service Corps and from the 8th October 1915 he served with the 36th (Ulster) Division Divisional Train which maintained a flow of supplies of stores and ammunition from the Base Depot Headquarters at Etaples to the front lines. He may have been selected for this duty due to his experience with accounting for shop stores and grocery deliveries gained in learning the process of running his father's business.

A series of events sealed Thomas' fate and ensured that he rejoined his original company, 'D' Company at the front line. On the 24th March 1916, after working for nearly six months

20 *Belfast News Letter*, In Memorium, 6th May 1920

with the Army Service Corps, Thomas was injured and started the journey of a casualty, being admitted to a casualty clearing station on the 30th March before the seriousness of his injury eventually caused him to be admitted to Base Hospital at Etaples on the 11th April 1916. There he made a recovery and on the 28th April 1916 he was deemed fit enough to return to duty. He did not however return to the logistics work he had been doing on the Divisional Train, instead he was sent back to his original Y.C.V. 'D' Company, now on the front line at Thiepval. Just one week later he was dead. Thomas Martin attended Donegall Square Methodist Church in Belfast and was also a member of St. Matthew's Church Total Abstinence Loyal Orange Lodge No. 880. He was the youngest son of Samuel Alexander and Frances Jane Martin who had had nine children, three of whom died at an early age prior to Thomas' death. Thomas was 22 years old at the time of his death. Two years after his death in, 1918, his father passed away.

EDWARD ADAMS

Until 1914 Edward Adams was a pattern maker at the Harland and Wolff works in Belfast's docklands. He lived at 32 Cullingtree Street in Belfast with his sister Ellen, his parents and other siblings having emigrated some years earlier. Edward had an active social life around Belfast prior to the war. He was involved with the Belfast Y.M.C.A. and was a member of the J.H. Sterling Masonic Lodge, No. 345 and also the King William Temperance Loyal Orange Lodge No. 369. On joining up with the Young Citizen Volunteers he was appointed to 'D' Company. After his deployment to France, while the 14th Battalion were operating close to the village of Varennes, Edward was evacuated to the base hospital with dental problems. He remained in hospital until 31st March 1916 when he rejoined his company, then employed in holding the front line trenches at Hamel, just across the

River Ancre from Thiepval Wood. It was here where he would meet his fate five weeks later. On the night of the 5th/6th May 1916 Edward found himself close by Lieutenant Walker when the bombardment of the wood began. As the bombardment intensified he narrowly escaped being buried in the front line trench when it collapsed, killing and injuring his colleagues. He immediately helped to try to free his buried mates but was killed a short time later alongside his Lieutenant, Jerome Walker, when a shrapnel shell exploded above them both. A few days after the bombardment in Thiepval Wood Lieutenant Monard, who had written the 'Incinerator' account of his last words to Lieutenant Walker, wrote a letter to Edward's sister. An extract from the letter was later published in the *Belfast News Letter*. The Lieutenant wrote:

> 'Your brother was killed early in the morning. The bombardment we were enduring was simply terrific and the trench held by your brother and his platoon was the most difficult and dangerous, and therefore the position of honour in our line. The shells continued to blow in the trench and kill the men on Private Adams' right and left for nearly two hours, but your brother courageously stuck to his post and refused to leave it. He was in close attendance to Lieutenant Walker, his platoon officer, when a shrapnel burst over their heads killing both of them. He died in the execution of his duty to King and country and his name will never die in the battalion. We are proud of him in his achievement.'

THOMAS GEORGE SLOANE

Thomas Sloane originally came from County Armagh. In civilian life he worked as a clerk at Young and Hyde Limited, linen manufacturers at Bedford Street in Belfast having previously served an apprenticeship there. Thomas lived at 9 Elswick Street with his older brother Hubert, sisters Martha and Harriet, mother Eliza and father Benjamin who was a shoemaker. The family had originally lived in Armagh City. Both Thomas and Hubert were original members of the Young Citizen Volunteers from 1912 at the time when it was a civilian organisation before the outbreak of war.

Thomas was assigned to 'D' Company on joining the 14th Royal Irish Rifles. His brother, Hubert, also enlisted in the army and was serving with the 9th Battalion of the Royal Irish Rifles as a Corporal. Without him even being anywhere near that part of the front line, the bombardment on the night of the 5th May 1916 was to have a shocking impact on Hubert Sloane. While serving with the 9th Battalion he became injured and was evacuated home. During this time he applied to be transferred from the 9th Battalion to the Young Citizen Volunteers in order to serve alongside his brother. Hubert's transfer was approved and he officially left the 9th Battalion Royal Irish Rifles on the 2nd May 1916 on transfer to 'D' Company, the same company as his brother Tom in the 14th Battalion. Hubert arrived with the 14th Battalion on the 14th May, 1916. He was oblivious to the fact that his brother was dead and indeed already buried at Authuile Cemetery. One of the first things he did on arrival with the 14th battalion was, quite understandably, to seek out his brother. There is no doubt that Hubert had been buoyed by the thought that from that point on he would fight the war alongside his older sibling, helping and looking out for each other. He was immediately met with the bleak reality of facing the war alone and having to come to terms with his brother's death. The event, unimaginable to us today, was recorded by Lieutenant Monard in the Y.C.V. trench newspaper, 'The Incinerator'. This event must have dealt a heavy blow to the morale of 'D' Company and to the all those who witnessed Hubert Sloane's arrival. The horrors of war were beginning to take their toll on the Young Citizens. Much worse of course was to come.

Thomas Sloane was 26 years old when he was killed in action.

DAVID THOMAS McKEOWN

David McKeown was well known to Jimmy Scott. He was the only member of Jimmy's 'B' Company to be killed on the night of the 5th May. Prior to the war he worked as a tram conductor, along with Jimmy, with the Belfast Tramway Company. He, like Jimmy, had moved to Belfast from a country town, in his case Dromara, County Down, seeking employment with the Belfast Corporation and associating himself with the Young Citizen Volunteers. While in Belfast he stayed with his uncle, also called David, at 46 McClure Street. David McKeown was part of 'B' Company Lewis gun section; when the bombardment began on the night of the 5th May he assisted in providing covering fire out of Thiepval Wood while those members of the Pioneer section, under Sergeant T. Murphy frantically tried to dig out those men who had been buried. David McKeown was along with 'B' Company Lewis gunner, W. Townsley, when a mortar shell exploded close to them, killing David McKeown instantly. Townsley was later awarded the Military Medal for his actions that night, an award which, unfortunately for the family of David McKeown, could not be made posthumously. An extract from a letter sent to David McKeown's father from his section commander appeared in the *Belfast News Letter*:

'Your son was on duty with his gun when a trench mortar shell exploded in the trench killing him instantly. Although only in my section a short time I had always found him to be a capable, willing soldier and also a good comrade. During the action he stood by his gun with great courage, and his name has since appeared in battalion orders for gallantry. To my assurance of great sympathy is added the sincere regret of his comrades in the section.'

David was 24 years old when he was killed.

JOHN STANLEY LOWE

Lance Corporal John Lowe came from Kidderminister in Worstershire. His father, Charles, worked in the carpet trade as a commercial traveller. John had an elder sister, Winifred, and a younger brother called Ernest. At the time of his enlisting in the 14th Battalion John gave his address as 13 Norwood Avenue in Southport in Merseyside. He was attached to 'D' company and was killed in action on the night of the 5th May 1916 at Thiepval Wood.

John Lowe was a member of 'D' company Lewis gun section. He had been promoted to Lance Corporal on the 1st May 1916, just four days before his death. He was 19 years old. Very little information exists on John Lowe save that he may have been employed as a steward on a ship operating between Liverpool and Belfast during 1914. He appears, from examination of records available, to have been an original member of the 14th Royal Irish Rifles, enlisting in September 1914. It may have been the case that his ship had docked in Belfast at that time and he took the opportunity to enlist there and then at The Old Town Hall in Belfast, a short walk from the docks. His family later lived, or perhaps owned, the Station Hotel in Harrogate as this is the address recorded for him with the Commonwealth War Graves Commission. In April 2012 the author, while carrying out research at Authuile Cemetery where John Lowe is buried, noted that a small Australian flag had been placed on his grave. The cemetery register showed that his grave had been visited by Michael Lowe from Sydney, Australia. To date attempts to identify and contact Michael Lowe have proved fruitless.

GEORGE TOLLERTON

George Tollerton was a married man who lived at 40 Mary Street in Belfast. He was originally from Coronation Street in Portadown, County Armagh. He was a member of 'C' company, being a Lewis gunner in that company. A letter to George's widow from his commanding officer was also published in the Belfast newspapers once news of his death was received:[21]

> 'During a very heavy bombardment of our trenches, and while he was on duty with his gun team, a trench mortar bomb exploded in the trench, killing him instantly. He was buried the following evening. Although only in my section for a short time, I had formed a high opinion of his abilities as a good soldier, and I had occasion several times to observe his coolness under fire. During the bombardment he stood by his gun with great courage and his name has since appeared in battalion orders for gallantry.'

The entry published reads remarkably similar to that printed referring to Rifleman McKeown. On studying the records today it is apparent that most of those killed on the night of the 5th May were in fact buried alive. The officer writing the letters spared the horrific details of the soldiers' deaths from families and loved ones. He was most likely unaware that extracts from his letters were being printed in the Belfast and local newspapers for all to see. Similarities in their structure and content would become apparent to those loved ones scanning the casualty lists for snippets of information in the same way that those similarities are apparent when researching the same publications today.

George Tollerton is remembered today on the memorial of Magheragall Parish Church near Lisburn.

JAMES WALKER

James Walker was a footballer; prior to enlisting he played for South End Rangers, Linfield Swifts and Linfield F.C. having played on their County Antrim Shield winning side. He continued to play football with the Y.C.V. and played in their 'C' Company F.C. team. He came from the townland

---

21 *Belfast News Letter*, 22nd May 1916. 'U.V.F. Casualties'.

of Clady near Dunadry in County Antrim. On that 5th May night James was pulled from the collapsed trench still alive. He was rushed down the casualty evacuation route out of Thiepval Wood to the dressing station at Authuile. From there he was taken by field ambulance to the field hospital at Forceville, a small village some six miles from the front line. There he died of his wounds on the afternoon of the 6th May 1916. His grave is at Forceville Cemetery today where it is regularly visited by members of the Linfield F.C. supporters club. Jimmy Scott recorded him as being buried at Authuile Cemetery along with the list of others killed that night. This was the first of a number of anomalies I discovered when exploring the circumstances in which the men named on the list were killed. James Walker was photographed just after his enlistment when he had begun training at Finner camp. On closer examination it can be seen in the photograph that James is actually wearing his football boots along with his civilian clothing, prior to the issue of uniforms.

GEORGE KIRKWOOD

James Walker wasn't the only footballer to lose his life as a result of the 5th May bombardment. George Kirkwood came from Alexandra Park Avenue in Belfast and played for Brantwood F. C. George and James obviously got off on a good start during training as he was also photographed with James in the early days at Finner Camp. George Kirkwood was a member of 'B' Company and was also injured during the bombardment. Like James Walker he was evacuated to Forceville where he eventually succumbed to his wounds and died on the 9th May 1916. He was also buried at Forceville Cemetery, in the same row of graves close by his comrade in sport, James Walker. George Kirkwood had played for the Y.C.V. 'B' Company F. C. team when they won the Regimental Cup competition in 1915. The team was photographed and the photograph published in the *Belfast Evening Telegraph* on the 7th June 1915.

George Kirkwood can be seen third from left in the back row. George Kirkwood's grave at Forceville was photographed by Corporal George Hackney, a photographer who served with the battalion and was a fellow member of 'B' company. Hackney remarkably compiled a photographic record of the men and the locations where they served throughout training and into the war. The unique grave design shows the high regard in which George Kirkwood was held by the men of 'B' Company. Hackney took two photographs of the grave, showing the later addition of the unique Y.C.V. cross which was specially made by the men of the battalion for each of their fallen. As can be seen from George Hackney's photographs the Y.C.V. cross differed considerably from the standard cross, showing that even in remembrance the Young Citizens differed from the norm.

THOMAS GRAY

Rifleman Tom Gray had also suffered serious injuries during the bombardment. He was evacuated out of Thiepval Wood to Forceville Casualty Clearing Station. From there, on the 12th May, he was taken by field ambulance to Etaples and then by hospital ship to England where he was admitted to the Military Hospital in Bath. Thomas finally died from his wounds on the 23rd May 1916. His body was returned home to Belfast and he was laid to rest in his family plot at Drumbo Holy Trinity Church close to his home at Ballycoan, Purdysburn, on Friday the 26th May 1916. A funeral procession had carried his remains from the Great Northern Railway station in Belfast. Thomas Gray was 23 years old.

Thomas Gray also served alongside his brother Alex in the 14th Royal Irish Rifles. Alex however had originally joined the 16th (Pioneer) Battalion and without doubt his pioneer skills were put to use on the night of the 5th May when he would have frantically dug out the dirt and rubble of the collapsed front line trench in order to try to save his older brother's life. In circumstances similar to those of the Sloane brothers, Tom and Alex Gray had taken steps in order that they should serve together. On the 5th August 1915 Tom Gray wrote to his commanding officer in the 14th Battalion requesting a transfer. He did not however ask that he be transferred out of the battalion but rather strangely, he requested that his brother Alex be transferred from the 16th Battalion into the 14th. The application was approved by Captain Samuel Willis, the officer in charge of 'D' company, acting on behalf of the commanding officer. Alex Gray continued to serve with the Y.C.V. until, on the 1st July 1916, he was injured by shellfire and knocked unconscious. When he regained consciousness three days later he found himself in a field hospital with no recollection as to what had happened to him. As a result of his injuries he was eventually medically discharged from the army suffering from epilepsy and rheumatism and the effects of shell-shock. He returned home to Ballycoen on the 22nd January 1917. Captain Samuel Willis, who had kindly recommended Thomas' request, was later killed during the 1st July attack leading his men at the third German line, over a mile in front of the British front line at Thiepval Wood. His body was never found. In December 1917, as a result of enquiries made through diplomatic Red Cross channels, his colleague Lieutenant Gracey, who had been taken prisoner on the 1st July 1916, described his final moments in a letter to the War Office while he was a prisoner of war in Germany.[22]

> 'Sir, In reply to your enquiry as to the fate of my brother officer, Captain S. Willis of the 14th Batt. Royal Irish Rifles, missing since 1st July 1916 I regret to state that I am unable to give any further particulars, save those I sent home from Germany while in hospital there and sent by my people to Mrs. Willis.
>
> While assisting to consolidate in the afternoon of the 1st July at "The Crucifix" in the German lines I received

---

22 National Archives, Officer's File, Capt. S Willis, WO 339/68266

an urgent verbal message from Captain Willis of our 'D' Company for reinforcements at a place called "Omagh", on my left on the road from Thiepval to Grandcourt. This place "Omagh" was over a mile from our own front line in the 3rd German main line of defences. I went to Captain Willis immediately, having reported to my senior officer at the Crucifix that I was going to do so. As I neared "Omagh" Captain Willis met me and cautioned me to keep my party (10 men) well down in the communication trench at the side of the road as we were under direct observation from Grandcourt. Captain Willis was talking with a Major (who was killed on 1st July) when I last saw him. My impression is that he had come forward from the 2nd German line behind us to establish communication with parties of the 107th Brigade at Omagh. We all took shelter in a German dug-out at this place from a small howitzer bombardment at about 5 o'clock in the afternoon and when this ceased took up our positions as beforehand. The counter-attacks came almost immediately and when I looked I found I was in command as I could not see Captain Willis or the Major (I don't know his name). I have come to the conclusion that Captain Willis at this juncture had once more gone back trying to establish communication with the rear as we had been trying to do during the day. I was knocked out a few minutes after this and I never saw Captain Willis or heard anything further of him since, in St. Quentin or Germany.

I need hardly say that if Captain Willis had been near me at the attack I would certainly have heard or seen him, acting as he always did, absolutely fearlessly and perfectly coolly and capable in the face of danger.

I have the honour to be, sir

Your obedient servant.

R. V. Gracey, Lt. R.I.R.'

THOMSON GOULD

Perhaps the most extraordinary story of those injured on the 5th May is that of Rifleman Thomson Gould. Thomson Gould was born in Belfast in 1896 and had lived at Olive Street and later at 14 Rutherglen Street. Before the war he worked for the Anglo-American Oil Company at their offices in Belfast. Thomson was 17 years old when he enlisted with the 14th Royal Irish Rifles in September 1914. On the night of the 5th May Thomson was caught in the bombardment at Thiepval Wood along with the rest of 'D' Company. Early in the bombardment, when the trench collapsed, Thomson found himself buried up to his neck and trapped. Horrifically he was forced to endure the whole of the bombardment in that position, unable to move until freed by Sergeant Tom Murphy's pioneer section once the bombardment ceased. He spent a short time at the field hospital before rejoining his section some days later.

On the 1st July 1916 Thomson Gould was involved in the attack at Thiepval along with the rest of his section. He again found himself injured and trapped in the 'Sunken Road' 100 yards or so into no-man's land in front of Thiepval Wood. Here, injured, he once again had to remain and endure the battle that carried on around him, this time for four whole days and nights. After the attack the Royal Army Medical Corps (R.A.M.C.) officer attached to the Y.C.V. battalion, Lieutenant Noel John Hay Gavin became aware that there were a number of wounded men still lying out in no-man's land. He organised a party of volunteers who once again made their way across the Ancre river and up through Thiepval Wood. There, on the night of the 4th July, they left the front line trenches and made their way into no man's land and the 'Sunken Road' led by the R.A.M.C. Lieutenant. Signaller William McCormack was in the party of men selected to carry out this task.[23] He

---

23 Diary of William McCormack, 'Keep Smiling', Nancy McCormack-Schaalje, Family Collection.

wrote in his diary that the battle was still raging along the front at Thiepval Wood. Lieutenant Gavin returned in the early hours of the 5th July after recovering a total of twelve men from the 'Sunken Road'; one of these fortunate men was Thomson Gould. On this occasion Gould was sent to the Base Hospital. His injury was recorded in the battalion casualty record as 'shell shock'.

Thomson Gould's war did not end there. On the 16th July 1916, showing extraordinary resilience, he rejoined his section, now with the battalion at Boisdinghem in northwest France, close to the border with Belgium. Here the men trained before they were put back into the line in the Messines sector in Belgium. While in the Messines sector Thomson carried out duty in the Ploegsteert area. On the 25th August 1916 he was manning a position known as Trench 131 which ran along the edge of a fortified farm, renamed earlier in the war as Seaforth Farm. Thomson was along with two new reinforcements to the battalion, brought in with a number of others late in July to help make up numbers lost, Rifleman John O'Hara from Ballymote in County Sligo and Rifleman Athay from Saffron Road in Bristol. At around 10.30am two shells exploded in Trench 131 right beside Thomson and his two new colleagues. John O'Hara was killed outright and Rifleman Athay died hours later of wounds. Thomson Gould survived the explosions and was evacuated to a field hospital suffering from shell shock. He remained in hospital and on discharge re-joined the battalion on the 15th September 1916 in trenches known as 'Cooker Farm'.[24] At 8.15pm that same evening Thomson was caught up in yet another enemy bombardment; this would be his last. He was injured once again and evacuated the next day to the field hospital before being sent on down the evacuation route. He was eventually returned to base hospital on the 17 November 1916 and then to hospital in England on the 10 December 1916. Thomson

---

24 National Archives, 14th R.I.R. War Diary, WO95/2511/1

Gould was discharged from military service three months later on the 5 March 1917. The note on his record states simply 'Sickness'. Thomson's battles did not however end there. He met and married Ellen Devlin in 1921. In 1922 she gave birth to their daughter Stella Doris Gould and they set up family at a new house on the Ballygomartin Road in Belfast.

Thomson could not settle; in 1924 he decided to emigrate and travelled to Canada leaving his Ellen and baby Stella in Belfast. He initially joined his sister Jessie at her home in Jones Avenue, Toronto, where he found work as a packer at the T. Eaton and Co. department store, a business founded in 1869 by Timothy Eaton, an Ulster Scot immigrant. Ellen and his daughter then joined him in Toronto and in 1928 they had a son called James. By this stage in his life Thomson had begun to show signs of what would today be diagnosed as post traumatic stress disorder. He was drinking heavily, by all accounts an alcoholic. One evening at around the time his son had just turned two years old Thomson left his house in Toronto, telling his wife Ellen he was 'just nipping out for cigarettes'. He was never seen again.

We can only speculate as to his fate but it is obvious now that his horrific recent past and that constant exposure to trauma got the better of him. He could not cope with a normal life; indeed his boundary markers of normal were far removed from anyone who had not lived through his experiences. His actions understandably caused ripples that reverberated down the generations. Ellen found that she couldn't cope alone with two children to the extent that one was put up for adoption, a horrific prospect today, splitting the family. Indeed to this day his descendants, unaware of the traumatising experiences that he had endured in France and Belgium, had written him off as a waster and scourge on the family. They now look on his past with at least some sympathy. His move to Canada was perhaps an attempt to break free of the demons and faces of the ghosts that continually crawled back and tugged at him from the bloody Sunken Road and putrid water of Trench 131.

3

Evolution

THE COUNTDOWN TOWARDS the inevitable so-called 'Big Do' slowly ran down for the remainder of May 1916. The men of the 14th Royal Irish Rifles began to discover clues to their eventual fate as they marched on a daily basis to the brigade practice area at Clairfaye from their billets at Lealvillers. There they practiced bayonet drills, rapid wiring, consolidating positions and attacks on a series of trenches that replicated those opposite the British lines at Thiepval Wood. Captain Alan Mulholland, the Adjutant and keeper of the battalion War Diary, recorded the following entry on the 13 May 1916, just three days into the training and commenting on the work he recorded on being informed that the proposed sector at which the battalion would attack was Thiepval Wood:[1]

> 'It all seems so simple and above ground. I don't think we quite realise what is before us'.

The level of training steadily intensified over the period of a month, building from section and platoon attack training to company level attacks, finally culminating in brigade level exercises taking place between the 7th and 9th June. This involved all four regiments of the 109th Infantry Brigade training together at a larger training ground near Warloy, some six miles west of Albert. On the 13th June training ceased and the men were moved to Aveluy Wood. Their work changed from training to carrying munitions and supplies and digging reserve trenches within Thiepval Wood. As the days passed the pressure on the men increased.

---

1 14th R.I.R. War Diary, National Archives WO95/2511/1

The battalion suffered only one casualty during this period. On the afternoon of Saturday the 17th June 2nd Lieutenant Frances (Frank) Corscadden was found seated in front of his bivouac in Aveluy Wood suffering from a gunshot wound to the head. He had been writing at the time. He was taken immediately to the field hospital of the 92nd Field Ambulance but died of his wounds the following day. Frank Corscadden had been a platoon commander in 'A' Company; he was 25 years old and had been a clerk in civilian life having previously graduated from Trinity College in Dublin. He came from Manorhamilton in County Leitrim, initially enlisting with the 14th Royal Irish Rifles as a Private soldier on the day the battalion was formed, the 14th September 1914, and had originally been attached to 'C' Company. His potential as an officer was observed early in his training and on the 30th January 1915, just after the battalion had moved from Bundoran to Randalstown Camp in Antrim, he was recommended for a commission by none other than the battalion commander Lt. Colonel Spencer Chichester. On completion of his officer training he returned to the 14th Royal Irish Rifles and took command of No. 1 platoon in 'A' Company. There appears to have been a certain amount of speculation amongst the men surrounding the circumstances of his death. Aveluy Wood was some distance from the German lines, perhaps a mile and a half or two miles away depending on where the men were positioned within the wood, certainly beyond the range of any sniper. John Kennedy Hope in a diary entry wrote:[2]

> 'We have a casualty in the wood before we leave it. A mysterious happening. A platoon officer of our company, Corscadden is found dead on a wicker seat where he is sleeping. It is thought he is the victim of a stray bullet from an aeroplane.'

Frank Corscadden was recorded in the battalion records

2 Diary of J.K. Hope, R.U.R. Museum

as having died of wounds on the 18th June 1916. He rests in Warloy-Baillon Cemetery close to the training area where the 109th Brigade had been practicing their attack.

The following day, Monday the 19th June 1916, 109th Infantry Brigade Order No. 50 was issued. This document detailed the order of battle for the coming offensive. The 14th Royal Irish Rifles, one of four infantry battalions that comprised the 109th brigade, were ordered to attack at Thiepval as part of the second wave assault in support of the 10th Royal Inniskilling Fusiliers who made up the first wave of the attack. These two battalions were to form the left flank of the attack on the 109th Brigade sector with the 9th Battalion of the Royal Inniskilling Fusiliers supported by the 11th Royal Inniskilling Fusiliers making up the right flank. No time for the attack had been indicated, only that the attack would take place on 'Z' Day and would be preceded by five full days of artillery bombardment of the German lines opposite Thiepval Wood and along the front. The artillery bombardment, designed to soften up the German positions, destroy the barbed wire entanglements that surrounded their position and penetrate the hardened bunkers which had been dug deep into Thiepval Ridge, was directed to commence on the 24th June 1916. This day was designated 'U' Day in the brigade orders and marked the first of five days solid bombardment prior to the planned attack date. The day of the attack, 'Z' Day, was to be Thursday the 29th June 1916. At some point on Tuesday the 27th June, 'X' Day, Jimmy Scott wrote his will into his soldier's pay-book.[3] Most men were either instructed to, or chose to, fill in the will page of the book before they deployed to France but Jimmy had waited until this point in the war to do so. Perhaps his confidence began to waver on witnessing the bombardment that fell along the front and he started to realise the vast power of the killing machine that modern warfare had become. His

---

3 National Archives of Ireland, Soldier's Wills, NAI/2002/119, E/309820/1

years of experience of open warfare in South Africa meant nothing when compared with the confinement of trench warfare combined with the wall of steel and lead, the like of which he had witnessed for three days, that could fall with no sign of abatement on an enemy, and therefore, at some point possibly on him. Industrialised warfare had come of age and Jimmy Scott was in the thick of it.

Four days later, on the morning of Saturday the 1st July 1916 the 36th (Ulster) Division attacked the German positions at Thiepval Ridge with the 14th Royal Irish Rifles, directing their advance from Thiepval Wood towards the trenches that made up the Schwaben Redoubt strongpoint. Jimmy Scott fought with the No. 7 Platoon men of 'B' Company. The early stages of the battle were recorded by the photographer and soldier George Hackney, the same man who had photographed Jimmy at Randalstown and Seaford the previous year. A few hundred yards away from Jimmy his brother, Edward, serving with the 13th Royal Irish Rifles, fought with honour and during the day carried wounded men back from the Sunken Road which ran across the battlefield back to the British lines at Thiepval Wood. He did this on no less than ten occasions and was later recommended to receive the Distinguished Conduct Medal. His award was eventually downgraded to the Military Medal. Edward Scott's heroic actions were replicated time and time again across the battlefield by the men of the division as they engaged in individual personal battles, many of which we shall never learn the detail of. The plight of the 36th (Ulster) Division during the action on the 1st and 2nd July 1916 has been recorded and documented many times during the past century. The day has widely been recognised as being the worst day in the entire history of the British Army. The figures speak for themselves with records from the Commonwealth War Graves Commission (C.W.G.C.) showing total fatalities for the 1st and 2nd July 1916 as 19,918 killed. This figure includes 12,974 men initially recorded as having been 'missing' on those two dates and recorded as such on the Thiepval Memorial to the Missing and having no known grave. These figures of course represent the losses across the entire allied forces for the dates stipulated. At a battalion level the proportion of dead and missing amongst the total casualties depended to some degree as to where the particular unit was deployed along the front. The 14th Royal Irish Rifles suffered a total of 99 men killed in action or died of wounds on and during the week following the 1st July battle; of these a startling 70 men are recorded as 'missing' and, to coin a War Office phrase of the time, 'died on or since' the 1st July 1916. The official battalion War Diary records total casualty figures of dead, wounded and missing as a cold percentage figure of 42.6% from a fighting strength of approximately 980 men. On the 2nd July a note entered at 2pm in the War Diary records what must have been a pitiful sight for Adjutant, Captain Alan Mulholland who recorded the following:[4]

> 'Thiepval Wood 2.7.16, 2.0pm...Battalion moved out across the South Causeway in single file about 120 strong, only two of the original officers of those who went over the parapet with it, Lt. Monard and Lt. Hogg – the former slightly wounded.'

On the 5th October 1915 on landing at Boulogne the battalion had numbered 29 officers and 995 men.[5] The once proud Young Citizen Volunteers had been decimated to an extent way beyond the Roman meaning of the word. Back home, across the counties of Ulster in the weeks that followed, newspapers began to publish desperate pleas from anxious mothers, fathers and wives seeking information of the whereabouts or fate of their young men, grasping desperately at any shred of information that might support the proposition that their loved ones could be alive, perhaps

---

4 14th R.I.R. War Diary, National Archives WO95/2511/1
5 Ibid.

as a patient in a field hospital or at worst a prisoner of war in a German compound. As time passed, and the grim reality finally dawned, for many the best that they could hope for was that their loved one was found in a marked grave and their name removed from the long and lengthening list of The Missing.

Jimmy Scott survived the battle physically unscathed; the 14th Royal Irish Rifles battalion was taken out of the line and the job of re-constructing the battalion from drafts of reinforcements began with the first draft of 45 men assigned to the battalion on the 2nd July, five more waves of reinforcements were assigned between the 2nd July and the 5th September 1916, totalling 365 men and 24 officers. The majority of these were inexperienced men who joined the battalion directly from training units.[6]

On the 27th July Jimmy Scott was promoted to Acting Company Sergeant Major and transferred from 'B' Company to 'D' Company within the battalion. This promotion was ratified and he was confirmed in the post of Warrant Officer, second class (WOII) the following week, on the 9th August 1916. At this time the battalion had moved to the Ploegsteert sector of the line near Messines in Belgium. Along the front at Ploegsteert the men settled once more into the routine of front line, reserve positions and billets. Jimmy's notebook remained as he had left it back in May; the task of recording the result of such a mass slaughter and entering the names of those lost or missing as a result of the 1st July battle was obviously too much. On the 1st October 1916, Jim was granted Home Leave for a period of four weeks, a particularly long period of absence but possibly due to him obtaining The King's Warrant on promotion. The battalion had been relieved at 4pm the previous evening on the front line at Cooker Farm by the Inniskilling Fusiliers and on a 'Beautiful autumn day with nothing to report' as described in the War

6 14th R.I.R. Battalion Casualty Record, R.U.R. Museum.

Diary, Jimmy Scott started on his journey home to Belfast. He carried the little notebook with him with the next pages populated with a further list, not of men killed and grave locations, but of names of men and their addresses back home. He had decided to share his valuable time on leave between his family and the families of those with whom he had served. Unfortunately we cannot know what messages or stories he had planned to pass on, but we do know the fate that had become the men whose loved ones he called with; in one or two cases we know more than he knew then. In one case in particular he could never have imagined the role that the occupant was to play in helping the nation come to terms with loss. In any case we can say that Jimmy's mindset had changed. He had decided to concentrate his efforts on the living. His list reflected this change; it had evolved from being a record of the dead.

MRS. J CAMPBELL
33 1/2 William St. Newtownards

Rifleman John Campbell no. 6712 had lived with his wife Nora and young son at William Street in Newtownards, County Down. He joined the 14th Royal Irish Rifles as part of the battalion's first reinforcement on the 16th December 1915 and was assigned to Jimmy Scott's 'B' Company. Both men had been tram conductors with the Belfast Corporation before the war, hence the inclusion of his name in Jimmy's notebook. Following the 1st July attack at Thiepval John was reported as 'missing in action'. Nothing was heard about him until the 5th July when he was found to have passed through the 108th Field Ambulance clearing station before being evacuated to hospital for further treatment. When Jimmy called at William Street in Newtownards in October 1916, John's family would have been aware that he had survived the battle. John returned to the battalion on 23 May 1917. He was in action again just two weeks later at the battle of Whytschaete, on the 7th June 1917, and was once again wounded. He was evacuated to the Richmond Hospital in Dublin on the 12th June. John succumbed to his wounds some four weeks later, on 14th July 1917. His body was brought to Belfast by rail and by cortege to Dundonald Cemetery outside Belfast where he was interred on 17th July. The burial took place with full military honours; he was 28 years of age. John's wife Nora passed away in 1988 and was laid to rest with her husband in the same plot at Dundonald.

MRS. NEVINS
13 Mcclure St.

John Nevins had lived at Powerscourt Street before moving to 13 McClure Street in Belfast, a street where he had originally grown up in and where he met his wife Emily Evans. John's first address on McClure Street was number 127, on his marriage to Emily Evans he moved into her family home at no. 13. John was a mechanic at the outbreak of war and had been a member of the original Young Citizen Volunteers since 1912. He enlisted with the 14th Royal Irish Rifles and was assigned to 'B' Company as a Sergeant with Jimmy Scott. John, like his friend Jimmy, had come through the 1st July battle unscathed and like his friend was also promoted to Company Sergeant Major rank whereupon he was transferred to 'C' Company. When Jim called with Emily in October 1916 she was mourning the death of her brother, Joseph Evans. Joseph was a Chief Petty Officer in The Royal Navy on board H.M.S. *Hampshire* when it was sunk by a German mine off the Orkney Islands during a storm on the 5th June 1916 with the loss of almost all of the crew. The sinking of H.M.S. *Hampshire* struck a heavy blow to the morale of the nation as on board was Lord Kitchener, the British War Minister, along with his staff and officials from the Foreign Office who were en route to Russia as part of a diplomatic mission to outline military policy to the Russian Tsar. Joseph

Evans left a wife, Annie and a young son, Norman.

John Nevins remained with the 14th Royal Irish Rifles until the battle at Whytschaete on the 7th June 1917 when he was injured by a shrapnel wound to his back. On convalescing he returned to service with the 1st Battalion of the Royal Irish Rifles and then later with the 15th Battalion. He survived the war and took up employment with his father-in-law as a glass cutter.

MRS. SMITH
94 Hamilton Road, Bangor

Jimmy's next trip took him to Bangor in County Down. Once there he made his way to Hamilton Road where he called with the family Rifleman Albert Smyth. (Name spelt Smyth in military records). It is unclear whether Jimmy found the family there as a second address of 20 Antrim Road, Belfast was recorded against the name. The Smyth family had links to North Belfast with previous addresses around the Antrim Road area. Albert, like Jimmy a member of 'B' Company, had also survived the battle on the 1st July. On the 13th September 1916 he was transferred to the 109th Brigade Trench Mortar Battery for what was termed as 'Special Duty'; this meant duty in connection with gas warfare.[7] Albert Smyth was killed in action at Langemark on the 16th August 1917, joining the ranks of The Missing with no known grave. He is remembered on the Tyne Cot Memorial to the Missing close to Ypres in Belgium. He was 22 years of age.

MRS. BRANKIN
10 Seventh Street, Shankill Road, Belfast

Sergeant George Brankin also served with Jimmy Scott in 'B' Company of the 14th Royal Irish Rifles. He was photographed relaxing on his bunk by war photographer and Y.C.V. Corporal George Hackney at Randalstown Camp in

7 Ibid.

County Antrim during initial training when he was a Lance Sergeant, a rank he had been given on joining the battalion. He was promoted to Sergeant on the 4th November 1914 and remained with 'B' Company. George was wounded during the 1st July attack and was evacuated away from the front, spending time convalescing at Ballykinlar Camp in County Down. George was originally a Newtownards man, living at 59 Frederick Street in the town, although he had lived at 54 Fifth Street Belfast on enlistment and later at 10 Seventh Street in East Belfast with his wife Mary. George returned to the battalion on the 30th April 1917 and was involved in the attack at Whytschaete on the 7th June 1917 where he was mortally wounded. He died of his wounds the following day at a casualty clearing station at Hazebrouck in Belgium and was buried nearby in the Communal Cemetery there.

R.H.
5 (1) Abingdon St.

Rifleman Robert Hanna of 'B' Company is recorded in company records as having lived at 5 (1) Abingdon Street in Belfast. Robert was appointed Lance Corporal on 1st May 1916, remaining with 'B' Company. He was wounded during the 1st July 1916 and evacuated through the 108th Field Ambulance casualty route to a base hospital on 5th July. The extent of his wounds is unclear; needless to say he did not re-join the 14th Royal Irish Rifles but did return to the front with the Royal Flying Corps. He survived the war.

HARRISON

Samuel Harrison was a Corporal in 'B' Company. Originally from Downpatrick in County Down, he gave his address on enlistment as Riverside Terrace, Old Hillsborough Road, Lisburn. Samuel had been a clerk in civilian life. Little is known of him and his relationship with Jimmy Scott other than being a Corporal in the same company and had being

promoted to Corporal just before Jimmy's visit on 23rd
September 1916. The following year, on 24th June 1917 he
was wounded by shell-fire at Whytschaete and evacuated
home. He was eventually discharged from service due to his
wounds on the 20th June 1918.

MURDOCK
39 Haypark Av.

Two Murdock brothers served with Jimmy in 'B' Company;
one, Ross was a Sergeant and the other, Albert a Corporal.
Their address was in fact 39 Hyde Park Avenue in North
Belfast which indicates that Jimmy may have enquired about
their address before taking his leave and been told by word
of mouth. In any case neither brother had been with the
battalion since 1st July; both were wounded. During the
battle Albert had been attached to the 109th Brigade Trench
Mortar Battery under the command of Captain Charles
McMaster, an original Y.C.V. officer. The men of the battery,
all originally 14th Battalion men, distinguished themselves
in the fierce fighting involved in taking the heavily fortified
position, the Schwaben Redoubt on Thiepval Ridge, where
they used their Stokes Mortar shells as hand held grenades
to blow in the German dugout doors. Ross Murdock was
discharged from service due to his wounds on the 19th
March 1917; his brother Albert re-joined the battalion and
was wounded again on the 23rd June 1917. On his recovery
he joined the 16th Royal Irish Rifles and survived the
remainder of the war.

McCOMB
10 River Terrace, Cook St., Ormeau

Lance Corporal Charles Barclay McComb, also of 'B'
Company, was reported missing in action on 1st July 1916.
He was eventually located in hospital with word passed to his

battalion on the 16th July 1916.[8] Following his recuperation
he was commissioned back into the Royal Irish Rifles as a
2nd Lieutenant before finally being officially discharged from
army service due to illness in May 1919. He married the
following year; tragically though his wife passed away in 1929.
Charles later re-married and was employed as an insurance
official. He died in 1960 at his home in 18 Lyndhurst Gardens,
Belfast.

MACKEY
5 Pier View Terrace

John Joseph Mackey enlisted with the 14th Royal Irish Rifles
at the outbreak of the war. He was a clerk in civilian life with
the shipping and marine insurance company W. McCalla &
Co. of Victoria Street in Belfast. John lived at 5 Pier View
Terrace in Holywood, County Down with his wife Ellen
and young son William, who was six years old in 1914. One
week after enlistment John was appointed Sergeant in No.7
platoon, 'B' Company along with Jimmy Scott. In fact he
appeared in a number of photographs with Jimmy, most
notably the 1915 Tug o'War team group photograph taken at
Randalstown Camp during training in early 1915.

A few weeks after the battalion's deployment to France John
was promoted to Company Sergeant Major and transferred to
'A' Company. John fought in the main significant battles with
the battalion, the 1st July 1916 attack at Thiepval and the 7th
June 1917 battle at Whytschaete before being wounded and
sent to a base hospital on 10th August 1917. John recuperated
at home until he was fit to return to the front on the 14th
August 1918. By this time the 14th Royal Irish Rifles had
been disbanded as part of a divisional re-structure so John
joined the 1st Battalion Royal Irish Rifles as Company
Sergeant Major; at that time the 1st Battalion were part of
the 36th (Ulster) Division having joined the division that

8 Ibid.

February. John was involved in the final actions of the war during what became known as the 'hundred days' offensive. The German Kaiserschlacht or 'Operation Michael' spring offensive had run out of momentum and Marshal Foch as allied commander had taken the opportunity to go on the offensive. By October 1918 the Germany Army in Belgium was in retreat. Pursuing them east of Ypres was the 36th (Ulster) Division with J.J. Mackey and the 1st Royal Irish Rifles. On 14th October the 1st Royal Irish made an attack on the village of Gulleghem, just north-west of Kortrijk, in an attempt to unseat the German positions there and push west. Fierce resistance was offered up from fortified positions resulting in The Rifles suffering a number of casualties, particularly among the officers. The action lasted two days and during this period Mackey's experience shone through. John was awarded the Distinguished Conduct Medal (D. C. M.) on the 21st November 1918. The citation, published in The *London Gazette* on 2nd December 1919 outlined his actions:

> '18393 C.S.M. J.J. Mackey, 1st Bn. R.Ir.Rif. (Holywood, County Down) During our attack on Gulleghem on the 14th October 1918 he rendered invaluable assistance to his company commander by reorganising the platoons and getting them into their proper positions after officers had become casualties. On the 15th October, after the village had been captured, he collected stragglers and formed a platoon which he personally conducted and placed in position on the final objective, during which time he was under heavy enemy machine gun fire. He exhibited great courage and coolness throughout the operations and by his example gave the men confidence and urged them on.'

During the action, over the two days of the 14th and 15th October, the 1st Battalion, Royal Irish Rifles suffered one officer and 27 men killed with six officers and 116 men wounded. The dead were laid to rest in Dadizeele New British Cemetery; nine men remain missing in action and are remembered on the Tyne Cot Memorial to the Missing.

It is difficult to gauge today how the fighting men perceived events that were unfolding in the political battle with Germany during these final days of the war, or if they had any knowledge at all of the impending end to hostilities. On the ground the Germans were making the allies fight for every inch they gave up. It is of course impossible to place oneself in the mind of insurance clerk John Mackey, after four years of terrible fighting and with a wife and now ten year old child at home in County Down, to find himself constantly pushed to the edge of existence where the very act of survival drew deep into reserves of pure courage. Just over three weeks later, at 2300hrs on the night of the 10th November 1918 with the battalion in reserve positions at Mouscron in Belgium, official news of the signing of the Armistice by Germany was received. The battalion buglers sounded 'Cease fire'.[9] J.J. Mackey's war was over. John was demobilised on 10th February 1919, he returned to Holywood and immediately left along with his wife and son for Canada where he settled in the town of Sproat near Revelstoke in British Columbia. John's Distinguished Conduct Medal was not forwarded to him until January 1922. John passed away just two years later on the 11th April 1924 at 37 years of age after suffering bronchial problems as a result of exposure to poisoned gas. He rests in Arrowhead Cemetery near Revelstoke, British Columbia, Canada.

CLARKE

Three men with the surname Clarke served in the 14th Royal Irish Rifles, the name in Jimmy's notebook most likely referred to Rifleman Donald Richard Clarke (name spelt Clark in later records) born in Dundalk, County Louth.

---

9 1st R.I.R. War Diary, National Archives WO95/2503/3

When war broke out he was living at his family home at 'Woodside', Ravenhill Road in Belfast; a later address was added to his record of 56 Cromwell Road in Belfast.[10] Donald had enlisted with the 14th Royal Irish Rifles at the age of 19 years and had been employed as an apprentice manufacturer in the clothing trade in 1914, having previously studied at Belfast Mercantile College. He was appointed to 'D' Company in the battalion, the company that Jimmy Scott took over on his promotion as Company Sergeant Major. Donald fought with the battalion at Thiepval on 1st July 1916 and was promoted to Lance Corporal on the same date. He gave a good account of himself during the action. His efforts on the day were recognised by his senior non-commissioned officers and on the 17th July 1916 he was put forward for a commission, his application being recommended by Captain Mulholland of Donaghadee, County Down and Captain Hanna of Newry.[11] The application was ratified by Brigadier General R. Shuter 'In the field' who stated that on the 19th July 1916 'I have seen this candidate and concur, after he has completed one month's course of training at a cadet school'. Donald attended No.2 Cadet battalion at Pembroke College, Cambridge and was formally discharged from the 14th Royal Irish Rifles on 27th March 1917 on being commissioned as a 2nd Lieutenant in the Royal Munster Fusiliers.

2nd Lieutenant Clark, as his surname now appeared, although appointed to the Royal Munster Fusiliers, was attached almost immediately to 'A' Company of the 2nd Battalion of the Royal Inniskilling Fusiliers, part of the re-shaped 36th (Ulster) Division. On the 21st March 1918 Donald's battalion was over-run at a strong point called 'Boadicea Redoubt' south of Grugies at St. Quentin in France after being subjected to the most ferocious artillery bombardment seen up to that point in the war. This bombardment marked the start of the German spring Kaiserschlacht Offensive which

10 14th R.I.R. Battalion Casualty Record, R.U.R. Museum.
11 National Archives, 2/Lieutenant Donald Richard Clark, WO 339/69452

ultimately marked the beginning of the end of the war, not before a heavy toll was inflicted on the allied troops. Donald Clark was taken prisoner and held until after the armistice, arriving back in England on 18th December 1918. Donald was interviewed in order to establish the circumstances of the surrender of his unit. A statement was recorded from him which best describes the events of the morning of 21st March 1918. The statement dated the 3rd February 1919 reads:[12]

'Sir, the company was holding a strong point or keep south of Grugies on the left of the St. Simon, St. Quentin Road. On the morning of March 21st a heavy fog lay over the ground. On the opening of the enemy's bombardment the above position was fully manned. Sometime afterward the bombardment eased a little and about 9am the C.O. Lt. Col. Lord Farnham, the 2nd in command and adjutant came into the keep. It was then that I received the first information about the enemy. They were at B.H.Q. (Battalion Headquarters) some 100 yards away and closing round us.

The fog was thick at this time and it was impossible to ascertain his position or movements but his machine guns were frequently heard. Towards noon the fog lifted. The S.O.S. Was put up, the C.O. Sent runners out to try and get in touch with other units (all other means of communication were cut with front, flanks and rear earlier in the morning). Nothing was heard of the runners again. In the afternoon great numbers of the enemy troops were observed in our rear moving in extended order and close formation in the direction of Grand Seracourt. During this time the enemy made several attempts to break through our defences on the right with bombing attacks but failed. Later in the evening a German officer with a white flag entered one of our posts. The Commanding Officer was immediately sent for. A conference of all

12 Ibid.

officers was called and after taking everything into consideration it was the opinion of most that we should perhaps in very short time be forced to give way, so I was thus taken prisoner with the others. The men fought with great spirit throughout the day.

I am, Sir, your obedient servant, D. R. Clark 2Lt.'

German accounts of the action and surrender highlight the gravity of the situation Donald Clark found himself in. Lord Farnham, an experienced and highly decorated soldier, realised that the game was up. Rather than waste the lives of some 250 brave men, who had fought valiantly up to that point, he took up the offer of surrender made to him. The alternative was to have his position pounded by heavy artillery. The Germans recorded the surrender: '... a few minutes later, there filed out of the redoubt a Lieutenant-Colonel, carrying a small white dog, three captains, seven subalterns and 241 other men. Forty-one machine-guns and mortars were found in the redoubt. The British Lieutenant-Colonel asked for, and was given, a document stating that he had put up a good fight before surrendering.' (Martin Middlebrook, *The Kaiser's Battle*.)

The statements of all of the officers involved were examined and, following consideration of the evidence, Donald was informed of the result of the War Office enquiry into the matter on the 21st July 1919:[13]

'The Secretary of the War Office presents his compliments to 2nd Lieutenant D. R. Clark, The Royal Munster Fusiliers and begs to state that he is commanded by the Army Council to inform him that his statement regarding the circumstances of his capture by the enemy having been investigated, the Council considers that no blame attaches to him in the matter. The investigation was carried out by a Standing Committee of Enquiry composed as follows:-

13 Ibid.

Major-General A.E. Price-Davies VC, CMG, DSO.
Brigadier-General C.R.J. Griffith, CB, CMG, DSO.
Brevet-Lieut-Col. E.L. Challenor, CB, CMG, DSO.'

One can only imagine Donald Clark's reaction to being investigated, having a statement recorded and waiting until late in July 1919 to be informed that no blame was being apportioned to him for the saving of his life. Lord Farnham had most likely seen enough waste of young life throughout the years of warfare, he had placed a much higher price on the lives of his brave men than the perceived damage to his reputation. As a result of his decision Donald Clark was spared. He lived a long life. His great-nephew, Paul Clark, is a broadcaster and Ulster Television News reader in Northern Ireland who takes great interest in matters concerning The Great War and is understandably proud of Donald's service and contribution to the war. Paul was unaware until recently of his great-uncle's imprisonment as a prisoner of war, nor of how Donald's fate balanced on a moment in time when common sense prevailed.

FERGUSON
2 Collingmore Rd, Agincourt Av.

Lance Corporal Walter Ferguson lived at 2 Collingmore Road in Belfast, at the junction with Agincourt Avenue where his father ran a coal distribution business. Walter was also attached to Jimmy Scott's 'B' Company and was a member of No.6 platoon under Sergeant William Stephenson. Jimmy had no way of knowing, but at the time of his visit to Collingmore Road in October 1916 Walter was dead. He had been taken prisoner during the 1st July battle when his position was overrun by a German counter-attack. It is highly likely that Walter was wounded at this point as he was taken to a German military hospital at Caudry, a French town some 30 miles east of the Thiepval lines. There on the 8th July 1916 he died and was buried by the Germans in the town's Communal

Cemetery. His paybook was recovered from his body by the Germans and contained his will, written just two weeks previously on the 22nd June 1916. The paybook, along with details of his death, were forwarded to the British authorities via channels established by the International Commission of the Red Cross. Eventually, on receipt of a direction dated the 13th December 1916, his battalion casualty record entry was adjusted from 'missing 1/7/16' to 'Now officially reported on or since 1 July, killed'.[14] The effect of the use of official terminology used at this stage of the war in phrases such as 'on or since' describing the status of casualties is one that I will touch on later; suffice to say at this point they gave little comfort to families concerned for their loved ones. Family visits, like those recorded by Jimmy, depending on what information was imparted, could be viewed by family members desperate for news as manna from heaven. Where they sought hope from witnesses of the battle, they could also just as easily, on the back of an unguarded and well intentioned comment, plunge families into years of hell and torment.

CARSON

A name recorded on Jimmy's second list was simply written in as 'Carson' alongside three different addresses. Research from the battalion records held at The Royal Ulster Rifles museum in Belfast indicated that this referred to 2nd Lt. William John White Carson. William Carson was born in 1889 and had been a member of the original, civilian Young Citizen Volunteers before the war and held the rank of Company Sergeant Major in that organisation. He lived in Belfast in the north of the city at Old Cavehill Road and had been employed in his father's estate agent business. William enlisted in the regular army at the outbreak of the war and joined the 20th (Public Schools) Battalion of the

14 14th R.I.R. Battalion Casualty Record, R.U.R. Museum.

Royal Fusiliers at Epsom on the 17th September 1914.[15] The
reason for him joining this particular battalion is unclear but
may have been due to him attending college in Epsom at
the time. On the 8th December 1914 William applied for a
temporary commission, listing the headmaster of Dungannon
Royal School Mr. R.W. Bingham as one of his referees. The
application was signed off by Colonel Chichester and on the
30th January 1915 William was discharged from the Royal
Fusiliers as a Private and appointed 2nd Lieutenant in the 14th
Royal Irish Rifles in charge of No. 3 Platoon 'A' Company
with an additional responsibility as reserve machine-gun
section officer. William Carson continued to train with the
men of A Company during their time at Randalstown and
on to England and France in October 1915. On the 22nd
June 1916 at Aveluy Wood he received his orders to go into
action with 'A' Company in planned action at Thiepval. 2nd
Lieutenant Carson was last seen alive in action at 10.30pm on
the evening of the 1st July 1916 at the third German trench
forward of the 109th Infantry Brigade sector at Thiepval
Wood. When Jimmy Scott called with his father and crossed
his name from his list, William Carson had been missing for
three full months. William's father, also called William, was
only beginning to come to terms with this new devastating
phenomenon. The loss of an only son in combat was hard
enough, to learn of a violent horrible death and to try to come
to terms with loss from that point was difficult. In peace time,
the loss of a loved one is difficult to endure and accept. There
is mourning, a funeral and religious service and a gathering
of friends and relatives to comfort and console. In war there is
still the time of death, the time of notification, a point where
everything changes and perhaps a letter explaining that there
is a grave at a quiet place, away from the battlefield, a place
for pilgrimage and remembrance in a time of peace, later. For
William Carson senior the future held only years of torture,

---

15 National Archives, 2/Lieutenant William John White Carson, WO
    339/16742

recorded with cold efficiency in his son's personal file.

Jimmy Scott was not his only visitor; wounded friends recuperating in Belfast called with William, intent on passing on condolences and sharing tales of his late son. These visits, obviously well-intentioned, had the effect of dragging out the pain for William and adding doubt to the already tumultuous cauldron of his mind. Six months after Jimmy Scott's visit, on the 19th April 1917, William Carson received the following letter from the C 2 'Casualties' Branch of the War Office:[16]

> 'I am directed to inform you that it is regretted that no further report has been received concerning 2nd Lieutenant W.J.W.Carson, 14th Battalion, Royal Irish Rifles, reported missing 1st July 1916.
>
> It is regretted that it will consequently be necessary for the Army Council to consider whether they must now conclude that this officer is dead.
>
> Before this course is taken, however, I am to ask if you will be good enough to confirm the fact that no further news of him has reached you.'

It was obvious that the War Office wished to draw a line under the matter of Lieutenant Carson's death. Indeed, as the war progressed guidelines were laid down at Whitehall as to how long a period of time should elapse from when a man is first reported as missing until his death should be accepted and whether the presumption of death should be made on the basis of elapsed time alone if no other evidence exists. Initial minimum time periods were set in late 1915 at six months for officers and seven months for other ranks. This time period was later extended to twelve months and was based on the fact that at that point in the war all cases of surviving men had been heard of within a twelve month period.

Further news had however reached Mr. Carson. He had been visited by two colleagues of his son. Captain Stanley

16 Ibid.

Monard from Lombard Street in Belfast, who was wounded on the 1st July as a Lieutenant, remained at his post and was promoted to Captain the next day and Rifleman Saul Hanna from the Newtownards Road in Belfast, who was also wounded during the 1st July battle. An account of the action on the 1st July was passed to William; he in turn wrote back to the War Office outlining the information he had received:[17]

'Capt. Monard spoke to my son at 10.15pm on the night of the 1st July while in the 3rd German line. Monard then mounted the parapet making for the British lines and was wounded in so doing.

Private Cousins, one of his two messengers (Cousins and Shannon) was here recently and told me he was with my son during the day and up till 10.15pm on July 1st when he was told to retire to the British line which he did so successfully. My son was then unwounded. A few minutes later Cousins' brother, also of the 14th battalion saw him and he gave Cousins a chunk of chocolate and he (Cousins) enquired about his brother and was informed that he was well and was just making his way towards the British lines.

Private Hanna whom I saw some weeks ago... informed me that he saw 2nd. Lieut. Carson at 10.30pm on the 1st July and had been with him during the entire day, and at the hour stated was ordered to return to the British lines, and only when about 20 paces distant he was hit on the leg by the fragment of a grenade and he threw himself into a dug-out close by and remained there until the following afternoon (Sunday) about 4.0pm when the British re-took the 3rd German trench and removed him to the Base and cleared up the trench and in which my son's body was not found and it is asserted by Hanna that he must have been taken prisoner. Why he has not written (if alive) is the puzzling part of it, but only last

17   Ibid.

week a boy of my acquaintance (a Private) missing since October 1914 wrote to his mother 3 weeks ago stating that he was well and unwounded and the reason he had not written earlier was that his turn to write had just come, the numbers of prisoners being very large.'

William Carson went on to describe how it was believed that the men of the Ulster Division who had been taken prisoner on the 1st July had attempted to escape from their camp and had been prevented from writing home as punishment. It can be seen that he was grasping at every possible hope that his son could still be alive, even hanging on the rumours derived from the tales of the gallant action that the Ulster Division had fought that day. Far from drawing a line under the matter, the Army Council were now obliged to follow up the leads he had given them from the information he had gleaned from Stanley Monard, Saul Hanna and brothers Alfie and John Cousins from 131 Madrid Street in Belfast. William in his letter set out his stance in no uncertain terms:

'Should the Army Council conclude that 2nd. Lieut. Carson is Dead, they may do so, and proceed as is customary in similar cases, but such procedure while perhaps proper in the opinion of the Council, will in no way convince me of my Son's death, nor until the war was over and every Prisoner accounted for... My Son elected to do his duty, and joined the Public School Contingent, as a Private in September 1914, leaving an established remunerative business, and an only son.'

The following week the Army Council C2 Casualties Branch replied once more and informed Mr. Carson that if he did not accept his son's death at that time they would respect his wish and keep the matter open in the meantime. They informed him that they believed that no officer could have been held as a prisoner of war for so long without information being passed to the Army Council via diplomatic channels confirming so. The Army Council also requested from Mr. Carson the details of the soldier whom he had previously mentioned as having been held in Germany without the opportunity to write home. One of the rumours circulating the country, not just Belfast at that time, was that there were secret prisoner of war camps where men were being held and used as labour for the German war effort. Other stories surfaced and were passed around telling of men who hid among the French and Belgian civilian population. Remarkably, the information that William Carson had heard regarding the soldier who had only just made contact with his mother after his capture in 1914 was founded in fact and referred to the case of Farrier Sergeant Alexander Kennedy of the North Irish Horse.

Alexander Kennedy was born in December 1892 and lived at Tullyherron in Waringstown. Alexander enlisted as a reservist with the North Irish Horse in 1910. His battalion was mobilised the day after Britain declared war on Germany on the 5th August 1914 and he deployed to France with 'C' Squadron on the 20th August 1914. The official records attached to 2nd Lieutenant Carson's file pertaining to Kennedy stated that he was wounded to the right knee and had been admitted to a civilian hospital at St. Quentin, France, just ahead of the German advance. The officer commanding 'C' Squadron of the North Irish Horse reported him as 'missing' on the 26th August 1914. Alexander however had managed to elude capture and was given refuge by a French family. An article appeared in the *Belfast News Letter* on the 24th February 1915 indicating that his parents had received a letter from him stating: 'He was a prisoner in the hands of the Germans and was in good health'. At this time though, according to the International Commission of The Red Cross and official War Office documents released later, he was still at large. It is possible that a letter was smuggled out of France to serve two purposes; to ease pressure on the French family concealing him and to let his family know that he was alive. According to official records, Alexander Kennedy was eventually captured by the Germans on the 20th April 1916, still at St. Quentin. The circumstances of his capture are unclear but it is highly likely that he gave himself up to minimise punishment administered to the family hiding him by the Germans. The Germans subsequently tried him under Martial Law and sentenced him to death. This sentence was later commuted to 10 years imprisonment. He was initially held in a prison at Rheinbach before being transferred west to Cottbus, close to the present day Polish/German border. Nothing more was heard from him until a postcard dated 17/9/16 was received by Edward Dupri Atkinson, Archdeacon at Donaghcloney Rectory in County Down. Alexander had written that he was a prisoner of war and was being held in Cell 506 Strafawsthal, Rheinbach in Germany. It was highly unlikely that Alexander could have known at that time but Archdeacon Atkinson's own son had returned from Canada with the Canadian Expeditionary Force as a Private soldier having emigrated there previously. In September 1915 he was commissioned from the ranks and actually posted to the North Irish Horse. Word was quickly passed to the military authorities and Kennedy's status was changed from 'presumed dead' to that of 'alive' and a prisoner of war. He was eventually repatriated at the end of the war to the Port of Hull on the 22nd November 1918.

The news of Sergeant Kennedy undoubtedly gave William Carson great hope that his son could still be found alive but the military authorities were quick to dismiss any such thought. They wrote:

'There have been a certain number of similar cases of men missing in the first few days of the war before trench warfare started who have subsequently been rounded up by the Germans.

The Army Council have unfortunately no reason to believe, however, that any men captured in the fighting on 1st July 1916 could have eluded their captors in a similar manner and it would of course be more difficult for officers than for men. But as previously stated the Council are willing to defer further action in regard to the official acceptance of death for the present.'

Second Lieutenant Carson therefore remained missing. Time pushed on and on the 11th November 1918 fighting in France and Flanders ceased. William Carson's position regarding his son remained unchanged. If anything, he believed that the ending of the war could present further opportunities to uncover fresh news of his survival with the allied armies sweeping into defeated Germany and uncovering hitherto concealed secrets as previously occupied areas of France and Belgium were liberated. In July 1919, the third anniversary of his son's disappearance brought the matter to the forefront of his mind once more when on the 24th July 1919 *The Times* newspaper printed a short article stating that the British Government had decided to dispatch a mission to France and Northern Belgium to follow up on all enquiries relating to missing men. On the 28th July 1919 Mr. Carson again wrote to the War Office with a further request for any information that this 'McIlwrath Mission' may have uncovered.

The 'McIlwrath Mission'; referred to by William Carson was a special mission appointed by the War Office made up of General Sir Malcolm McIlwrath, General C.D. Bruce and headed by Dame Adelaide Livingstone. Adelaide Livingstone (nee Stickney) brought a wealth of experience to the mission, as an American citizen and Quaker she was opposed to war and from the outset of hostilities used her American citizenship to assist Belgian and indeed British women refugees caught up in the German advance and finding themselves behind enemy lines. Her work brought her in contact with Nurse Edith Cavell who was famously executed by the Germans for harbouring and aiding the escape of British troops hiding in

Belgium. Following her marriage in late 1915 Dame Adelaide Livingstone assumed the nationality of her husband and was from that point regarded as a British citizen and as such could no longer safely move across the lines in Belgium and France. She continued her humanitarian efforts and used her valuable contacts to try to establish the fate of prisoners of war. This work evolved again when she later became an assistant to the Department of Graves Registration And Enquiry, a department which we shall hear of later, established to identify and record the many graves left on the battlefields of France and Flanders once hostilities ceased. Dame Adelaide Livingstone described her early work in an Appendix to a report of the General Committee Of The Treatment By The Enemy Of British Prisoners Of War dated the 23rd April 1920 as follows:[18]

'During the winter and spring of 1915, I went on behalf of the International Women's Relief Committee, to the occupied districts of Belgium and France in order to bring back English girls and Belgian children to this country. In the course of my work I travelled extensively in Belgium and met and spoke to many Belgian, French and English people who were employed in assisting English officers and men to escape. These officers and men had in many cases become wounded on the battlefields of Belgium and France during the early days of the war. They had succeeded in crawling away unseen by the Germans and had been in hiding in the houses of Belgian and French peasants and other residents. These people were assisted from place to place and ultimately through the help of Nurse Cavell and others succeeded in escaping to England.

I saw myself while in Belgium in April 1915, a party of some 200 men who were at that time escaping. I further

18 National Archives, Germany: Prisoners: Draft Appendices for the Report of the Independent Committee on Prisoners, FO 383/499.

visited the houses of several Belgian subjects, where officers or men had been concealed. In the convents of the neighbourhood were also, in some cases, cellars where our men had been hidden. A certain number of records were kept and I was informed by the Mayor of Mons that after the war he and other prominent citizens of Mons would be prepared to hand over records, letters and discs of men who had died whilst they were being nursed and concealed by the Belgians. One of the people who gave me this information was arrested with Nurse Cavell, and sentenced to 15 years solitary confinement in Germany. This man's evidence should now be available.

In May 1915 notices were placarded all over the towns of Belgium and France stating that any inhabitant found hiding an English officer or soldier would be liable to be shot.

It is possible that many officers who were in hiding at that date gave themselves up when these posters appeared and it is probable that these officers were shot by the Germans as spies and that no record of their death has ever reached this country. It is also known that when Nurse Cavell was arrested some officers were caught hiding in her house, and in the houses of those who were in league with her. It is probable that they were shot, and it is improbable that their names were sent through to England. In several cases Privates have turned up as prisoners in Germany a year or more after they were declared missing. These men had been in concealment in Belgium or France, and had, after many months given themselves up to the Germans. They were placed in military confinement by the Germans for a time, and afterwards drafted in ordinary camps. No officers have so turned up, and it is probable that they were shot when they gave themselves up, or when they were caught. In the course of my duties as Honorary Secretary of the

Government Committee on the Treatment by the Enemy of British Prisoners of War, I have had certain statements made to me, most of which on investigation proved to be unfounded, but a few of which should certainly be pursued now that facilities for investigating them further are at hand. I should suggest that when all the prisoners have returned to this country, and when all the sources of information in England have been exhausted, steps should be taken to get into touch with the many people in Belgium and France who sheltered our men at the beginning of the war.

It should then be possible to obtain the definite evidence of the death of many men now posted merely as missing. Though it is to be feared that no missing prisoners will prove to be still alive. Further the German Government should be asked to produce records of all officers and men who were found in concealment and shot.'

It was highly likely the case that William Carson believed that little was being done by the authorities between bouts of correspondence, as 1919 passed into 1920 his son's disappearance on the battlefield at Thiepval was no nearer to being reconciled in his mind. Life in Belfast had moved on, but all across the country William had joined the ranks of thousands of fathers, mothers, wives and sisters who were suffering the agony of having a family member declared missing in action, a term usually followed by the words 'on or since' and the date of a battle or action where men literally disappeared from the face of the earth. How could one just accept such a vague concept?

To their credit, it can be seen from the exchange of paperwork that the War Office followed up on all of William's enquiries. In late 1919 a report was received from Dame Livingstone's mission marked 'Not to be communicated outside the war office'. This report contained the names of three men forwarded to the mission for information and enquiry. Of the three names one man, 2nd Lieutenant A.F. Field of the Leicestershire Regiment had been found, buried in a lone grave near Le Cateau, the conclusion of the enquiry being that he had died while a prisoner of war in enemy hands, on or since 22 March 1918. The other two names on the sheet were that of Lieutenant T.H. Boswell of the Royal Flying Corps and 2nd Lieutenant W.J.W. Carson of the 14th Royal Irish Rifles. With the exception of the date added, the text of the report was identical for these two men, and for thousands of others:

> 'No further information has been received, and in the view of the lapse of time since he was reported missing his death has now been accepted for official purposes as having occurred on or since 1 July 1916.'

This report arrived on the desk of C2 Casualties Branch at the same time as William Carson's final piece of correspondence; which alluded to his thoughts that perhaps Private Saul Hanna, while trying to say the right thing, had sent William Carson on a four year journey into purgatory:[19]

> 'Sir, referring further to yours of July last, has any information been received directly or through Mr. McIlwrath's mission relative to my son... It seems strange that the War Office never received any information regarding him. The 3rd German trench in which my son was last seen at 10.30pm on 1st July 1916 was never out of British hands. Private Hanna of my son's platoon saw and spoke to him at 10.30pm and subsequently received a wound, from which he lay where he fell till Sunday afternoon when the British removed him and cleaned up the trench. Hanna asserts my son was undoubtedly taken prisoner.
>
> I would gladly know the worst, and it's really mistaken kindness by friends to withhold information should the

---

19 National Archives, 2/Lieutenant William John White Carson, WO 339/16742

worst have happened. I shall be glad of any information the War Office may have received lately. Should no tidings be forthcoming I suppose the Army Council will presume he is dead and will so advise, Poor Lad.'

William John White Carson's death was finally formally accepted by his father and his estate settled on the 15th March 1920. His death was officially recorded and the relevant details forwarded to his father using the now well used terminology 'as having occurred on or since the 1st July 1916 in either France or Flanders'.

4

Fitz, 172 Roden Street

ON THE 6TH November 1916 Jimmy Scott left a Belfast shrouded in winter and made his way back to Belgium. His period of leave, long as it was, had ended. He had made a decision to share his valuable time between those he loved and the loved ones of those with whom he had served. He knew only too well that fate could easily point her fickle finger in his direction. He had survived a terrific battle that had left his home city reeling and in mourning. Aside from the joy of seeing his wife and five children once more he had been confronted at every turn by grief. He rejoined the men of the 14th in Belgium at the Spanbroekmolen sector of the front line. He found his company in rest billets at a position called Derry Camp south of Lindenhoek, east of Kemmel Hill. Three days later he once again took up frontline positions around Cooker Farm at Spanbroekmolen and settled again into the routine of rotating in and out of frontline and reserve positions and training the waves of reinforcements that arrived to bolster his broken battalion. Over the following weeks the battalion slowly moved along the line, taking up ever new positions until in early January 1917 they billeted in reserve positions at Red Lodge and rotated in and out of the front line from La Plus Douve Farm, a headquarters position roughly 500 metres from the front line opposite German held Messines village itself. On the 22nd January the 14th Royal Irish Rifles relieved the 9th Royal Inniskilling Fusiliers at the front line.[1] As the relief was being completed, at approximately 3pm, a German

---

1 14th R.I.R. War Diary, National Archives WO95/2511/1

The graves of the men whose names were written into Jimmy Scott's notebook. *(Author's photograph)*

Jimmy Scott with Jane and family pictured in Belfast around September 1912. Jimmy is wearing a Young Citizen Volunteer lapel badge. *(Scott family archive)*

14th Royal Irish Rifles, No. 7 Platoon, in September 1915 at Seaford, East Sussex just prior to deploying to France. Sgt. Jimmy Scott front row seated, second from right. (*Scott family archive.*)

Rifleman George Dorrity
(Courtesy Pat Geary)

The graves of Sgt. William Stephenson and Riflemen George Dorrity, George Foster, William Henry Reid and Randolph Campbell at Hamel Military Cemetery, France. *(Courtesy of Dave Donatelli Collection)*

14th Royal Irish Rifles 'B' Company Tug of War Team, 1915. Sergeant William Stephenson standing second from left, arms folded, Sergeant J.J. Mackey far right, Sergeant Jimmy Scott forth from right, rear, RSM Robert Elphick left seated and Captain Harper centre. *(Scott family archive)*

Lieutenant Jerome Lennie Walker, killed in action on 5th/6th May 1916 at Thiepval Wood in France. *(Royal Ulster Rifles Museum Belfast)*

Rifleman David McKeown also killed on 5th/6th May 1916 at Thiepval Wood. *(Royal Ulster Rifles Museum Belfast)*

Rifleman George Kirkwood died on the 9th May 1916 of wounds received during the bombardment on the 5th/6th May 1916. *(Royal Ulster Rifles Museum Belfast)*

Lieutenant Frank Corscadden. Died as a result of a gunshot wound to the head in Thiepval Wood, France on 18th June 1916. *(Royal Ulster Rifles Museum Belfast)*

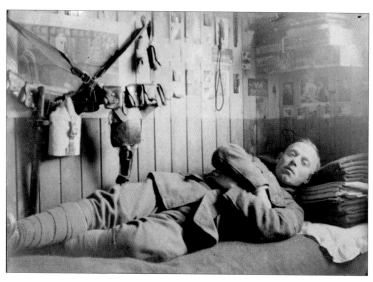

Sergeant George Brankin relaxing at Randalstown Camp, Co. Antrim. He died on 8th June 1917 of wounds sustained the previous day during action at Whytschaete in Belgium. *(Photograph George Hackney)*

Sgt John J. Mackey DCM. Died on the 11th June 1924 at Sproat near Revelstoke, British Columbia having suffered bronchial illness as a result of exposure to poisoned gas. He rests at Arrowhead Cemetery, Revelstoke, British Colmbia, Canada. *(Scott family archive)*

Lt William Carson. His death was finally accepted by his father in March 1920 as having occurred on or since the 1st July 1916 in either France or Flanders. He is remembered on the Memorial to The Missing of the Somme at Thiepval in France. *(Royal Ulster Rifles Museum Belfast)*

Major Samuel Ernest Sydney Fitzsimon M.B.E. known as 'Fitz'. *(Fitz-Simon family archive)*

Fitzsimons family group circa 1915. In uniform from left to right; Ernest, John (Jack) and James. *(Fitz-Simon family archive)*

Major Ernest Fitzsimon (centre) photographed at Belfast City Hall in November 1924. Jane Scott, widow of Jimmy Scott, 4th from left beside officer. *(Fitz-Simon family archive)*

Sergeant Jimmy Scott on horseback during weapon training at Seaford, East Sussex in September 1915 prior to deployment to France. Photographer was George Hackney. *(Scott family archive)*

7th November 1920 at Amiens Cathedral. Major Ernest Fitzsimon, centre (marked 'X'), Marshal Foch and General Phillipot left of him in image; Andrew Fisher in top hat with General MacDonogh and General Wyatt right of him in image. *(Fitz-Simon family archive.)*

Marshal Foch addresses the crowd at the quayside, Boulogne, 10th November 1920, with the coffin containing the body of the Unknown Warrior alongside H.M.S. Verdun. (© Imperial War Museum, Photographs Q70591)

HEADQUARTERS.   BRITISH TROOPS IN FRANCE AND FLANDERS.   "K"

Staff Duties - "Q" Branch.

Staff Officer: Major S. E. S. Fitz-Simon, M.B.E., D.A.Q.M.G.

Staff Captain: Captain C. J. T. Webb, M.C., R.F.A.
Staff Captain: Captain C. M. Smith, M.C., R.A.S.C.
Staff Captain: Captain D. Barry, M.C.

All Financial Questions (F)	Fires	Postal
Allowances (C)	Hirings and Requisitions	Stationery (C)
Accommodation	R.E and R.E. Stores (C)	Signals (D)
Ammunition	Transport, Establishment, etc (A)	Remounts (D)
Water	Water	Veterinary
Claims	Moves	Surplus Stores - Declaration of Camps
Courts of Inquiry	Railways and Roads	Surplus. Handing over
Canteens	Hutting	to Disposal Board.
Cars - Allotment of (A)	Secret Files	Voluntary Institutes.
D.G.R and E Supplies (A.B.C.)	Ordnance.	Relations with Inhabitants.
Establishments (except Infantry).		French Mission.

A	B	C	D	E	F	G
D.A.D.S & T.	C.R.E.	R.A.O.C.	D.A.D.V.S.	R.Signal Corps	Camp Comdt.	H.Q. Garage
	Major A.D.Spooner M.C.	Major H.Wheeler M.C.	D.A.D.T.	A.Major	Captain	Lt.E.G.Poole
	Major J.L. Thomas	Ordnance Officer	Lieut. Kidd	Lieut. Kidd	A.W. Smith O.B.E.	
	Captain C.L.M.Dowst R.E.		Major E.Norman		Lieut.C.L. Hardwicke	
	Captain S. Robinson R.E.					
	Lieut.Cook Jones Captain J.P.					
	Adams					
	R.E.Companies					
	etc.					
	M.T. Companies					
	Supply Sections					
	H					
	D.A.D.P.S.					

'Q' Branch D.G.R.&E. structure at St. Pol. (Fitz-Simon family archive)

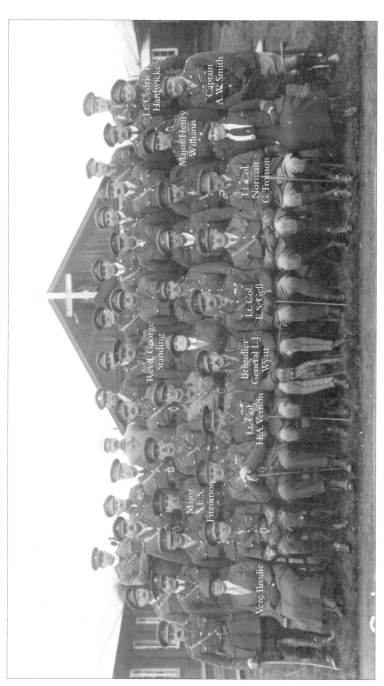

The officers of the D.G.R&E. At St. Pol. (*Fitz-Simon family archive*)

Vere Brodie, of Brodie, Nairn, Scotland served in France as a Volunteer Aid Detatchment (VAD) nurse before later taking charge of the Queen Mary's Army Auxiliary Corps unit at St. Pol where the selection of the Unknown Warrior took place.

LAST OF THE B.E.F. IN FRANCE

The last of the B.E.F. to leave the war area in France and Flanders. Major E. S. FitzSimon (centre), Lieutenant C. W. Hardwicke, C.S.M. Pratt and Lance-Corporal Parker. The tattered Union Jack on the car has seen seven years' service.

Miss Ivy Jenny, for the second year in succession, has won the City Corporation exhibition prize of £80 for violin playing.

Daily Mirror 28th October 1921 'Last of the B.E.F. in France.' *(Fitz-Simon family archive)*

Ireland Hockey Team at St. Pol. *(Fitz-Simon family archive)*

Cecil Smith, Fitz and Henry Williams.

Reverend George Standing, Lieutenant Cecil Smith, Lieutenant Henry Williams and Major Ernest Fitzsimon at St. Pol. *(Author's collection, courtesy of Janine Watrin)*

Major Ernest Fitzsimon's Identity Card. *(Fitz-Simon family archive)*

Cagnicourt British Cemetery *(Author's collection)*

The 'gap' at Cagnicourt British Cemetery in the third row of graves, left of centre of image. *(Author's collection)*

Major Fitzsimon circa 1921 at his brother Jack's grave, Connaught Cemetery at Thiepval in France. *(Fitz-Simon family archive)*

artillery barrage swept the front and rear positions just right of those taken over by Jimmy Scott's company. During this bombardment the company headquarters dugout received a direct hit. Jimmy Scott was inside the dugout at the time and was killed instantly by the explosion. His body was recovered from the smashed dugout by his men who carried him back to the rear position at La Plus Douve Farm. There he was buried with full military honours by the Reverend Captain James Gilbert Paton, a Presbyterian minister from Coleraine, who was awarded the Military Cross on three occasions before returning to civilian life after the war as Moderator of the Presbyterian Church in Ireland. Jimmy Scott rests at La Plus Douve Farm to this day. His effects were returned home to his widow Jane in Belfast; they included his Queen's and King's South Africa medals, a blood-spattered photograph of him with his family, a tin box of unopened cigars, and the diary which I was handed in April 2012.

The adventure that had been Jimmy's life was over. From the mills of Gilford to the great battles of Colenzo, Pieter's Hill and Ladysmith to gun-running with Major Fred Crawford and his time with the Ulster Special Service Force of the Ulster Volunteer Force, his days with the Young Citizen Volunteers which he had helped train from a civilian boy's club to a fighting battalion. For him, all was over. The war continued on, resulting in some of the men whose families he visited around Belfast the previous October being killed, or surviving the war, or remaining missing.

The concept of The Missing was something that Jimmy, with all his years of experience, could not have begun to comprehend. Jimmy had only witnessed the beginning of the suffering of families like that of William Carson; it is impossible to know if he had reconciled in his own mind the effect that the thousands of missing would have on a nation. Jimmy had witnessed the horrors of the 1st July at Thiepval when he was faced with the fact, as the days unfolded, that three quarters of his company were listed as missing. Surely he knew, after witnessing men blown to nothing, that the chances of any of the missing returning home were narrower than slim. He had the experience of the battle, of which there would be many more after his death and before the war ended. Unfortunately, the nation at home knew nothing of that experience and nothing upon which they could apply sensible reasoning or, as we term it today, closure to ease the grief they suffered.

There was one other name in Jimmy's notebook. It was written in a way that was difficult to decipher; the handwriting had been distorted in that it appeared that his pencil had been forced into the page part-way through writing the name as if his elbow had been nudged just as he put pencil to paper. There was an address beside the name, the main body of which I could easily read as '72 Roden St.'. Roden Street remains in part today; in 1916 it ran from the Donegall Road in South Belfast to the Falls Road in the west of the city. It was a working class area in 1916 and it remains a working class area today; with original terraced housing still standing. Today, however Roden Street has been cut in two by the Westlink Motorway that divides the city along both sectarian and geographical lines. The name beside the address appeared to read 'Fitzy' a nick-name applied to anyone in Belfast with a surname beginning with Fitz, like Fitzgerald or Fitzpatrick or similar. I searched the census returns and available street directories for 72 Roden Street but could not match a name to the address that warranted the nickname 'Fitzy'. I went back to the other names in the book and continued my research, occasionally returning to the Roden Street puzzle. On one such return, after maybe six months of poring over records, I happened to look at the writing from a different angle; it was at that point that I realised that the entry read 'Fitz, 172 Roden Street'. I had mistaken a number '1' for a letter 'y'. The research suddenly opened up. The family that had lived at 172 Roden Street was called Fitzsimons. A search in the 14th Royal Irish Rifles Casualty Record, held at the Royal Ulster Rifles museum in Belfast, revealed that three members of the battalion gave addresses at 172 Roden Street; they were James and John, both corporals along with Jimmy Scott in 'B' Company and a third brother, Samuel Ernest, whose name appeared in the officers section of the roll, spelt as Fitzsimon without the final 's'. The Fitzsimon family, as far as census records could indicate, had lived previously in Coagh and Aughnacloy in County Tyrone. The head of the family, Charles, who originally came from County Donegal, had been a constable in the Royal Irish Constabulary and on promotion to Sergeant rank had taken a position in Belfast which necessitated the movement of the family to Roden Street. Charles' wife Jeanie had come from America. They had four sons and four daughters. When war broke out both John, known also as Jack, along with James enlisted straightaway in the 14th Royal Irish Rifles. Jack was the youngest of the three brothers who joined up at 19 years, James was 20 and Ernest the oldest at 22 years in 1914. Ernest did not enlist straight away. In 1914 he had been studying at teacher training college under the Irish National Education Board at Marlborough Street College in Dublin. Over the summer of 1914 Ernest obtained permission from the Commissioners and School Manager at Marlborough Street to continue his studies at Queen's University Belfast and join the army in the form of the Queen's University Officers' Training Corps (O.T.C.). He returned to live at Roden Street and for over two years took up a position as an assistant teacher at Lomond Avenue National School in East Belfast. Ernest excelled in both, achieving a first place in the Officer Training Corps examination. In February 1916, on the back of a glowing report from Major Gregg Wilson at Queen's O.T.C. and from Mr. John McGaw, the principal at Lomond Avenue School, he was commissioned as a 2nd

Lieutenant in the 20th (Reserve) Battalion of the Royal Irish Rifles and sent for further training at Cork. Four months later, on the 20th June 1916, Ernest arrived at the front line in Thiepval Wood in France and immediately took up a position as Brigade Intelligence Officer at 109th Infantry Brigade Headquarters. Ernest had joined the battalion at the most intense point of the build-up to the 1st July battle. On that particular day the 109th Brigade Headquarters had moved into its Battle Headquarters position[2], a series of dugouts just south of Thiepval Wood itself. Ernest remained at that position until 5pm on the 2nd July 1916, when the brigade was relieved and the Headquarters re-established in Martinsart across the Ancre Valley. Ernest Fitzsimon had been dropped straight into a chaotic hive of activity as orders were passed on and received during the build up to the attack with men and equipment moving into position in Thiepval Wood then the wounded, signallers and prisoners moving the opposite way once the attack itself had begun. As Ernest worked in the dugout under artillery bombardment he was acutely aware that just a few hundred yards to his north his two younger brothers were in the thick of the action, exposed on the battlefield.

John 'Jack' Fitzsimons was killed in action that day. He had initially been recorded in battalion records as having been wounded; this occurrence must have been witnessed to warrant such a record. The record was then added to with the words 'Now Missing' and finally the entry in the casualty record was amended with the words 'Now Killed 1/7/16'. James Fitzsimons survived the battle, and the rest of the war. He was promoted to Sergeant with effect from the 1st July 1916 and was awarded the Military Medal for gallantry on the same date for his work as battalion signaller or 'runner'. It was his job to run with messages, in relays with other signallers, from the front line to the rear positions. The stress on each

---

2 Ibid.

of the three brothers during the build-up to the attack and during the day itself must have been incredible. In the days and weeks after the battle Ernest and James had to pick up and move on, carrying on in their separate but connected lives. We know now that Jimmy Scott had sad news to deliver during his visit to 172 Roden Street. There is no doubt that the visit was a difficult one. In the days following the battle the local newspapers carried conflicting news of the two brothers. The *Belfast Telegraph* published copies of their photographs along with the text:

> 'Corporals James and John H Fitzsimon, Royal Irish Rifles are sons of Mr. C.E. Fitzsimon, ex-Sergeant R.I.C. 172 Roden Street, Belfast. The former has been awarded the Military Medal and the latter is wounded and missing.'

The effect on Jeannie Fitzsimons lasted for many years, she could not accept the loss of Jack; the initial report of 'wounded and missing' introduced an element of doubt in her mind. Efforts were made by Ernest in later years to try to help her reconcile the death, indeed one result of her actions in not accepting the death was not properly resolved until over a century later.

In 2012 I managed via a chance internet contact to track down Dr. John Fitz-Simon, Ernest's son, who was living in Canada. I spoke to John by telephone and he was fascinated to discover that Jimmy Scott had noted and visited his father's address in Belfast in 1916. John told me what he knew of his father's service over a number of telephone calls before meeting me some months later in Belfast at the Royal Ulster Rifles museum. Along with him to the meeting John brought a large box of documents and photographs relating to his father. Ahead of this meeting I received a phone call from Linda McAuley, Ernest's great niece. Linda, a B.B.C. radio broadcaster in Belfast, had been in touch with her uncle in Canada and had found other items from the family archive at her mother's home in County Down. Linda confirmed that her Great-Uncle Ernest was known in the family as simply 'Fitz', the same nick-name that Jimmy Scott had written in his book. Linda then asked me if my great-grandfather had been a Sergeant and would he have been called 'Jimmy'. I confirmed that that was the case regarding his rank and that all I could say about him being called Jimmy was that it was a name that my late father was always referred to as, rather than James. When I asked why she was asking such pointed questions about Jimmy Scott the reply knocked me back. In April 1966, just before travelling to Thiepval in France to attend the 50th commemoration of the 1st July battle, Ernest had written to his brother James asking him if he could share reminisces or stories from the trenches. James sent two letters in response which give us a fascinating, detailed insight into trench life and the battle itself. My main purpose in researching the names in my great-grandfather's book was based on a simple line of thought; if Jimmy Scott took the time to write a man's name and address in order to visit that family, then would that man have taken the time to write about Jimmy Scott? Linda read from the letter, written 50 years after the fact, and my heart stopped. James Fitzsimon wrote to Ernest:[3]

> 'Thiepval, it is hard to remember incidents after over 50 years have passed, it was just routine from day to day. Somebody killed or wounded, like an Enniskillen (Inniskilling Fusilier) when we were firing our football mortars, they were about the size of a football with a long metal stem, the stems when the bomb exploded flew all over the place. The 'skin' was curious to see this and stood with his head over the parapet watching, the bomb exploded and the stem came back and practically took his head off.
>
> I don't think we grew callous about things but when Sergeant Jimmie Scott had just returned from cleaning

up after a mortar bombardment and we were having something to eat and talking about it (he) picked up a small piece of bread and said, "They were blown into pieces as small as this" and popped it into his mouth it was taken as a matter of course.'

To say I was shocked was an understatement. After a period of 50 years had passed, Jimmy Scott had been remembered from one brother to the other and furthermore, the incident referred to, the mortar bombardment, most likely related to the incident in May 1916 that caused Jimmy to record the list of names of the men killed in his book as he stood, after clearing up, at Authuille Cemetery not far from Thiepval Wood.

Jim Fitzsimons' letters went on to describe life before and during the battle:

'As you know I was in the trenches for a week before the attack and was supposed to go to the medical centre on the slope going down to the river (River Ancre) which was thought could not be shelled. Up to that point nothing had hit it. Thank goodness I did not go as the morning of the attack they wiped it out. The week before the attack the Germans saturated Thiepval Wood with tear gas. After a couple of days I became immune and did not notice it and made myself useful guiding working parties coming up with streaming eyes and practically blind. One night one fell in the trench in which I was sleeping and I had to put on my gas mask and I slept the rest of the night in it, a bag soaked in some chemical with a mica window in it, I slept.'

Of the day of the battle itself he recalled:

'I joined the batt when they arrived up morning of the 1st (I was supposed to go to the first aid post) and we moved into position. It was a nice dry day, slight mist early which soon cleared. We were all well laden with extra ammo and Mills bombs, some of the Inniskillings carried

Stokes mortars (used to blow open the doors of the deep German dug-outs). The 10th Inniskillings were the first wave at our section of the trenches and we followed, we had very few casualties. At the second German line we leapfrogged the Inniskillings leaving them to clean up. We halted half way between the second and third German lines as the third line was still being shelled by our artillery (we were a bit early I think). Met a hare between trenches, tempted but I did not shoot... we were now coming under heavy m/g [machine gun] fire and shelling of their own trenches. We dug in half way between the two lines but a Lewis gun team took up position in our funk hole so I moved 150 yards to the left and dug in again. Our artillery had ceased to fire and we could see the Germans in increasing numbers in front of us. I made my way to battalion HQ from shell hole to shell hole and after refusing a drink from the Colonel demanded he produce a map and get artillery fire where it was needed. Returned to German front line after a short rest but all was confusion and most retreating. Stayed there at the German first line until dusk. Returned to our front line and helped a first aid man in small shelter. Threw one soldier out for kicking up such a row, he only had 3 or 4 little wounds in his back as if someone had taken a teaspoon and scooped a few spoonfuls out. We had several very badly wounded to attend to. Then helped organise a line of defence in our second line trenches, difficult to keep the men awake. Batch of new young bewildered officers arrived to take over (not fair to them).

Jim Fitzsimons offered up his own explanation for the battalion not suffering large numbers of casualties during the early stage of the battle:

'I think my little section came out with so few early casualties because we were always a little ahead of the barrage times and we were able to catch the Germans before they had time to man their trenches from their deep dug-outs.'

The content of the letters was amazing but only the surface of the material produced by John Fitzsimon. One photograph produced from the collection showed Fitz with two other officers standing outside Belfast City Hall attending a remembrance service. As I studied the photograph I was shocked once again, this time to see a face that I recognised. Standing alongside Fitz were two ladies, solemn faced, in mourning waiting to lay a wreath. The face that I had recognised was that of Jane Scott, Jimmy Scott's widow, my own great-grandmother. I had recognised Jane from the blood spattered family photograph returned with Jimmy's effects. I studied the photograph in more detail, carried out research into it and discovered that it had been taken on Armistice Day in November 1924. I found a print of the same image in an archive copy of the *Belfast News Letter* which named the three officers as Lieutenant Colonel Sir William Allen DSO, Lieutenant Colonel S.E.S. Fitzsimon MBE and Captain J.H. Stewart.[4] The three men had laid a wreath during the Remembrance Service at the Belfast City Hall on behalf of the 36th Ulster Division Officers' Association. The photograph of Jane was positively identified by her youngest son to her second husband, again a part of the story had come around full circle. I suppose that when we look more empathetically at the photograph and place it, and her with Fitz, in context it was not surprising that she was there at Belfast City Hall on Remembrance Sunday in 1924. She had lost her husband and Fitz had lost a brother. From Jimmy Scott's diary entry we know that the two families knew each other. The three Fitzsimons brothers had each served with Jimmy Scott, a Sergeant and then Warrant Officer in the battalion, even Ernest as a newly commissioned 2nd

---

4 *Belfast News Letter*, November 12 1924, 'Belfast Honours The Memory of the Glorious Dead.'

Lieutenant would have always been advised not to ignore the veteran Company Sergeant Major's advice, so to see her in the same photograph as Fitz at that particular place and time was not so unusual. What was difficult for me to fathom was the fact that after following up a name written in a notebook in 1916 a man, John Fitz-Simon, should travel a century later from Canada and on meeting me produce a photograph of my great-grandmother.

John mentioned one more thing that would ultimately reveal hitherto unknown details of an event of national importance. An operation conceived at the highest level and carried out in secret but which addressed to a greater degree an issue upon which we have touched, that of The Missing and the effect that such massive loss had on the nation at that time. John said to me, in a casual manner, 'Oh, and after the war my father did that thing with the Unknown Warrior.'

5

Known Unto God

D R. JOHN FITZ-SIMON returned to Canada leaving the large archive of documents and photographs with his niece Linda McAuley in Belfast. Over the following months and indeed years I studied their content with the help of staff at the Royal Ulster Rifles Museum and remained in regular touch with John by telephone, letters and email. I was able to piece together Ernest Fitzsimon's military service history primarily from a curriculum vitae which he had prepared dated 1st June 1942. At that time he was a barrister, living in Dublin where he had settled with his wife Mabel Brittain after their marriage in 1928. Mabel had been a medical doctor in Dublin. It is not known why Ernest prepared the curriculum vitae at that time, in the middle of the second world war, or if any application connected with it was successful or not. The document itself was written with a particular slant to his various intelligence roles between 1916 and 1918. It can be seen from this document that for almost a year from the date of his appointment in France Ernest Fitzsimon performed the duties of battalion intelligence officer with the 14th Royal Irish Rifles. After the successful battle at Whytshaete on the 7th June 1917 he was commended for his skill in organising the signals and lines of communication from the frontline positions back to Brigade Headquarters. His organisational skills did not go unnoticed and he was selected and moved into intelligence roles at brigade level and from there into staff appointments. His educational qualifications were drawn upon when he reorganised the 109th Divisional Specialist

School in 1917.[1] His restructuring served as a model for specialist schools of instruction across the whole Second Army. In January 1918 he carried out the reorganisation programme within the Fifth Army whereby infantry brigades were reduced in strength from four to three battalions. Following the Armistice in 1918, Ernest was retained as a commissioned officer despite him being of 'temporary' rank, which was normally for the duration of the war only. He was awarded the M.B.E. in June 1919, having been promoted to Captain the previous month. The list of senior officers on whose staff he served in both Captain and Major rank was impressive and included Lieutenant General Sir H. Gough's staff with the Fifth Army, General The Lord Rawlinson's staff on two separate occasions with the Fourth Army and Field Marshal Sir Douglas Haig's Staff at General Headquarters of the British Expeditionary Force (B.E.F.). Later in the war and after the Armistice he remained in France serving on the staff of Brigadier General L. J. Wyatt and finally as Staff Major with the Headquarters British Troops in France and Flanders under Brigadier General J. K. Dick-Cunyngham. Ernest included as a reference on his curriculum vitae fellow Ulsterman Field Marshal Sir Archibald Montgomery-Massingberd of Gunby Hall, Lincolnshire.

One sentence in the document however jumped out from the page. Ernest had written:[2]

> 'Submitted and carried out the scheme for the selection of and removal of the remains of "The Unknown Warrior" from the "Field" to the destroyer Verdun at Boulogne'.

On reading this sentence I immediately thought back to what Ernest's son John had mentioned about his father being involved with the Unknown Warrior. At the time I had taken what he had said with more than just a pinch of

---

1 Curriculum Vitae, Ernest S. Fitz-Simon MBE, Fitz-Simon family archive, Dr. John Fitz-Simon, Canada.
2 Ibid.

salt. I had known the basics of the story of the Unknown Warrior and could vaguely recall that it had been instigated by an army chaplain called David Railton at the end of the war and that the selection of the body had been carried out in utmost secrecy; my knowledge on the subject at that time ended there. I started to examine the many documents and photographs that had been left by Ernest Fitzsimon with a renewed impetus; had Ernest Fitzsimon been linked to this important piece of our national history? Firstly, the curriculum vitae itself added weight to the proposition. It was highly unlikely that a barrister-at-law would make such a statement about a very public event if it was not actual fact, particularly in 1942 when many of those involved in the operation would still have been alive. But then again, I had nothing to say that the curriculum vitae had ever been submitted and Ernest's son had no knowledge as to the position it was used to apply for. I found both a typed copy and a handwritten original amongst the documents. I was still required to be convinced and continued looking for supporting material. An important find was Ernest Fitzsimon's identity card containing his photograph; it had a print date of June 1920 and had headings printed in French. It read, 'Carte D'Identite (Officier Anglais), Numero 279, Nom, Major S.E.S. Fitz-Simon MBE, Regiment, Royal Irish Rifles.' The card was signed by Captain J. C. Howard as Staff Captain for General Officer Commanding British Troops in France and Flanders and was countersigned by S. Batoy, Capitaine Le Chef Du Service de Liaison Francais. The photograph very clearly showed Ernest in Staff Major uniform; importantly this document gave me a sound point of reference that could be used to help identifying Ernest in other photographs. I then set about examining the large collection of photographs, all in black and white, of varying sizes and quality. One series of images showed a group of French and British officers walking at the head of a large group of people in front of the elaborately sculpted facade of a cathedral somewhere in France. One of these images had been annotated by hand with the names of some of those in the photograph. Fitzsimon was in the group, clearly now identifiable, but alongside him with names handwritten in ink were 'Foch', 'Fisher', 'Gen. Wyatt' and 'Gen. Macdonogh'. Marshal Foch was easily identified in the photograph even apart from the fact that a name had been affixed to his image, but of the others, 'Fisher' meant nothing to me as did Macdonogh; General Wyatt however had been mentioned in Fitzsimon's curriculum vitae. The location and the event were unknown. After reading a number of accepted accounts one thing became very clear. General Wyatt had been involved in the Unknown Warrior operation along with General Macdonogh, so Fitzsimon was photographed along with these men and Marshal Ferdinand Foch, the Supreme Allied Commander in France and Flanders, at the conclusion of the Great War. The significance of the series of photographs was still unknown but slowly more weight was being added to the idea that Fitzsimon was actually involved in the operation that his son had spoken of.

I next began to compare the frontage of the cathedral shown in the photograph with photographs of other large churches that I could find around France until I was satisfied that the view that was photographed was the western facade of Amiens Cathedral. This I confirmed on visiting the Cathedral. The scene which I photographed was practically unchanged. I had confirmed the identity of three of the men who were in the group of photographs and where they were taken but the identity of the man marked simply as 'Fisher' was unknown as was the date of the images and why the men were there. My focus then turned to newspaper accounts and after some painstaking searches I found an obscure paragraph in *The Times*[3] which reported on an event on the 7th November 1920 at Amiens. It simply stated:

---

3 *The Times*, 'Memorial to Fallen Australians' 8th November 1920.

126

'At Amiens Cathedral today a memorial to fallen Australian soldiers was unveiled by Marshal Foch', the report went on to state, 'among those present was Sir Andrew Fisher, the High Commissioner in London.'

I could then place the photograph in context, Ernest Fitzsimon had accompanied Marshal Foch, Generals Wyatt and Macdonogh and Sir Andrew Fisher, the Australian High Commissioner at an event to commemorate the Australian forces repulse of the German advance at Amiens in 1918. The date of the photograph and the event was Sunday the 7th November 1920, just four days before the body of the Unknown Warrior was buried in Westminster Abbey. Ernest was certainly with the right people at around the time and place to be involved, but what was his role? What exactly happened?

As the Great War progressed, particularly following the Somme battle, the immense loss began to be felt back at home. Attitudes to death had been rooted in the recent Victorian past when a death was expected to take place in bed, followed by the process of mourning, an outpouring of grief at a church service and a chance for family and friends to gather and support one another. There was an evangelical emphasis placed upon death as a moment of judgement. Loved ones at home, as we saw with the experiences of William Carson, were suddenly faced with the grim prospect of having no body at home to bury or even the report that, as far as could be established, no actual body existed at all. A church service, performed as a funeral without a body held a hollow meaning, adding to the grief felt and the dented morale of the population. A soldier's name and date of death added to an existing headstone on a family grave, as was what often happened, gave at least a point of remembrance, though hardly a significant one. At the front the role of the military chaplain in performing burials was extremely difficult. All prospects of an elaborate Victorian funeral could be forgotten about when the soldiers were living amongst the dead, who were buried often in makeshift graves close to the trench lines, exposed to the pulverising power of artillery that scattered body parts and grave markers alike across a cratered battlefield.

Against such a backdrop one military chaplain, the Reverend David Railton M.C., considered how the pain suffered by those relatives of The Missing could be eased. He came up with an idea to bring 'the body of a British Warrior unknown by name or rank to lie among the most illustrious of the land in Westminster Abbey'. The idea was first formed in his mind in early 1916. Years later, in 1931, David Railton described how he was inspired to come up with the idea when he wrote an article for inclusion in volume VII of the 'Our Empire' magazine titled 'The Origin of the Unknown Warrior's grave.'[4] In the article Railton described how he had returned from the front lines to his billet at Erkingham near Armentières in France. There was a small garden at the rear of the billet; a fallen soldier had been buried in the garden. The grave was marked with a small white cross and written on the cross in pencil were the words 'An Unknown British Soldier' with an addition underneath in brackets 'of the Black Watch'. David described how he wrestled with the idea of how this body could be brought back to 'ease the pain of father, mother, brother, sister, sweetheart, wife and friend.' David realised that in 1916, with the war raging, this was an impossible task. It was an idea however that he harboured until after the end of the war, when, in August 1920, he wrote to the Right Reverend Bishop Herbert Ryle, the Dean of Westminster and asked if he would consider the proposition of burying 'one of our unknown comrades' in Westminster Abbey. Two months passed, then came the reply:[5]

---

4 David Railton M.C. M.A. The Origin of the Unknown Warrior's Grave, *Our Empire* Vol. VII, 1931.

5 Ibid.

'The Deanery, Westminster SW1

Dear Mr Railton,

The idea which you suggested to me in August I have kept steadily in view ever since. I have been occupied actively upon it for the last two or three weeks. It has necessitated communication with the War Office, Prime Minister, Cabinet and Buckingham Palace. The announcement which the Prime Minister will, or intends to, make this afternoon, will show how far the Government is ready to co-operate. Once more I express my warm acknowledgement and thanks for your letter.

Yours sincerely Herbert E. Ryle, Bp. October 19, 1920'

Behind the scenes elaborate plans were put into place to facilitate the ceremony whereby the body of the Unknown Warrior was to be buried within Westminster Abbey. Armistice Day, 11th November 1920, had already been the focus of detailed planning as it was on this date that the newly completed Cenotaph was due to be unveiled. A temporary structure had been built to facilitate the Victory Parade in July 1919. This had become such an important focal point for mourning in the capital that it was decided to replace it with a permanent structure. Prior to Armistice Day in November 1920, this structure had been hidden from view by scaffolding and sheeting while the works were carried out with the unveiling to take place during the remembrance ceremony. A committee was set up within The Cabinet headed by Lord Curzon to initially plan the remembrance ceremony at the Cenotaph. His remit was then expanded to include the interment of the Unknown Warrior at Westminster Abbey. The planning for the entire public ceremony with the inclusion of the important new addition was completed within a period of just over three weeks. Lord Curzon, in the Cabinet Memorial Services Committee minutes debated and then outlined specifics relating to the selection of the Unknown Warrior body. Straightaway the numerous complexities of such an operation became apparent. With every aspect of the operation focused on inclusivity, the body had to be representative of any of The Missing; no section or element of society could be excluded nor could the origin of the body selected exclude any of the fallen on a geographical or chronological basis if it was known that the body was taken from a particular battlefield or from an area that was fought over at a specific point during the Great War. All that could be known was that the body would be of some British fighting man who had died for his country in the War. The committee discussed how the body should be described in that the word 'Warrior' should be used as opposed to 'Soldier' as this would exclude members of the Royal Navy who served as infantry or airmen of the Royal Flying Corps, later the Royal Air Force, who had in death joined the ranks of The Missing. The Adjutant General, (A.G.) General Macdonogh had an input on the Committee and had suggested that the body should be exhumed from a place where the Naval Division had fought alongside a Military Division. He further suggested that an initial proposal of the Committee that the body should be that of a man who had fallen in 1914 rendered this impossible, as the Naval Division did not take part in the operations in France until 1916.

What became very clear was that as much as the final procession and burial within Westminster Abbey was overt and very public the opposite applied to the initial selection process which had to be carried out covertly and with the utmost secrecy. The mourning public had to remain assured that the body finally buried within the Abbey could be everyone and at the same time any one of those men denied a proper identifiable grave by the misfortunes of war. This aspect of the operation became a matter for the Military Authorities. On the 22nd October 1920 a written order was sent from the Adjutant General's office in London to the Department of

Graves Registration and Enquiry (D.G.R.&E.) at St. Pol in France.[6] After all the discussion and debate the order itself was, on the face of it, quite succinct:

> 'UNKNOWN WARRIOR
>
> The following provisional instructions have been issued by A.G. in connection with the interment of "An Unknown Warrior" in Westminster Abbey on Armistice Day:-
>
> D.G.R.&E. will exercise his discretion as to location from which the body is exhumed.
>
> Date of original burial should be as far back as possible.
>
> Under instructions to be issued later, the body will be conveyed to Calais and there placed in a full sized coffin, which will be sent out from England.
>
> Sufficient soil is to be sent with the body to cover the coffin and fill a full sized grave.
>
> War Office
>
> 33-38 Baker Street
>
> Portman Square
>
> London W1
>
> 22nd October 1920.'

The officer to whom this document was sent was none other than General Louis John Wyatt, at that time the General Officer Commanding British Troops in France and Flanders and the Officer Commanding the army's Directorate of Graves Registration and Enquiry (D.G.R.&E.). He was identified in the photographs taken along with Ernest Fitzsimon at Amiens Cathedral on the 7th November 1920. The officer who issued the order was General George Macdonogh, the Adjutant General, also photographed in the same series of photographs with Fitzsimon. As I studied more of the documents in the archive it became apparent that Ernest Fitzsimon served with the D.G.R.&E. as a Major at their headquarters at St. Pol, the headquarters from where

---

6 Commonwealth War Graves Commission Archive file No. ADD 6/1/16, 1/11/1920–22/10/2009

the Unknown Warrior operation in France was co-ordinated. The Directorate of Graves Registration and Enquiry evolved from an earlier structure within the British Expeditionary Force called the Graves Registration Commission. This unit was responsible for the collection of information on British fatalities and the locations of graves. In 1917 the D.G.R.&E. was restructured again with mobile Grave Registration Units (G.R.U's) having areas of responsibility within each of the five Army areas. Each G.R.U. was typically commanded by an officer of Captain rank with two subalterns and squads of men to carry out exhumation and reburial work. Following the Armistice in November 1918 the emphasis of these units was to attempt to recover, identify and re-bury men buried in isolated graves and to concentrate small cemeteries into larger ones. This work also encompassed the reburial and attempted identification of The Missing, estimated to be in the region of half a million men. The work of the D.G.R.&E. was taken over by the Imperial War Graves Commission in November 1921[7] and the military exhumation parties were finally withdrawn from France and Flanders. The exhumation work was continued by civilian reconstruction gangs and local inhabitants re-working their land after the war. The Imperial War Graves Commission annual report for 1920-1921 gave an indication of the task involved in body recovery stating that 503,025 graves had been located and registered in France and Flanders out of roughly one million death casualties.

What appears to have been considered the definitive account of the Unknown Warrior operation was that which was published from a letter Brigadier General L. J. Wyatt wrote to the *Daily Telegraph* on 11th November 1939, nineteen years after the event. He began this account by stating that a number of accounts had previously been published but that what followed was the 'authentic' account of what took place.

7 Commonwealth War Graves Commission Archive file No. ADD 6/2/3,
  IWGC Annual Report for 1921-1922.

He further wrote:[8]

> 'In October I received a notification from the War Office that King George V had approved the suggestion and the proposal that the burial should be in Westminster Abbey on Nov. 11. I issued instructions that the body of a British soldier, which it would be impossible to identify be brought in from each of the four battle areas – the Aisne, the Somme, Arras and Ypres on the night of Nov 7 and placed in the chapel of St. Pol. The party bringing in each body was to return at once to its area, so that there should be no chance of their knowing on which the choice fell.
>
> Reporting to my headquarters office at St. Pol at midnight on Nov. 7, Col. Gell, one of my staff announced that the bodies were in the chapel and that the men who had brought them had gone. With Col. Gell, passing the guard which had been specially mounted I thereupon entered the chapel.'

Already in his account the emphasis was on secrecy; each exhumation party immediately returned to their specific area, not knowing the reason for their task or if others were involved. He continued:

> 'The four bodies lay on stretchers, each covered by a Union Jack. In front of the altar was the shell of the coffin which had been sent from England to receive the remains. I selected one and with the assistance of Col. Gell placed it in the shell, we screwed down the lid.

With regard to the three bodies not selected General Wyatt was quite specific:

> 'The other bodies were removed and reburied in the military cemetery outside my headquarters at St. Pol. I had no idea even of the area from which the body I had selected had come; No one else can know it.'

---

8 Brigadier-General Louis J Wyatt, Letter to the Editor, *Daily Telegraph*, 11th November 1939.

General Wyatt then described the events as the operation continued over the next two days:

> 'The following morning the Church of England, the Roman Catholic and the Non-Conformist chaplains held a service in the chapel. On the same day, at noon, the shell, under escort was sent to Boulogne, where it was placed in a plain oak coffin, with wrought iron bands, through one of which was passed a Crusader's sword from the Tower of London collection. While the coffin lay in the Chapelle Ardente in Boulogne Castle a company of French infantry mounted guard over it.
>
> The next morning, carried by the pall-bearers, who were selected from NCO's of the British and Dominion troops, it was placed on a French military wagon and under the escort of French troops taken to Boulogne Quay, where a British destroyer was waiting. The Admiralty had sent H.M.S. Verdun as a special tribute to the French nation and the gallant defence of that city.'

The General went on to describe how Marshal Foch and Lt.-General Sir George Macdonogh received the body at the quayside and made speeches before H.M.S. *Verdun* moved off carrying the body to Dover.

Ever since the date of publication of General Wyatt's letter it has been used as the definitive account of the operation; however when one attempts to piece together an event timeline to join the covert and overt aspects of what happened the dates simply do not add up. If the body was selected as stated at midnight on the 7th November 1920, then on the following afternoon, which was the 8th it was taken to Boulogne. There it remained, guarded for one night by French soldiers so the next day, when General Wyatt states that it was brought to the Quayside and H.M.S. *Verdun* at Boulogne brings, us to the 9th November. The body arrived at Dover that same day and was transported by train to Victoria station where it was guarded overnight, in the same railway

carriage used on two separate occasions to convey the bodies
of Nurse Edith Cavell and Merchant Navy Captain Charles
Fryatt, two civilians executed by the Germans. The following
day very publicly, it was brought to Westminster Abbey, but we
are still one day short. If we begin at the 7th November and
work through the events as stated we arrive at the 10th. If we
work backwards on the timeline, based on what we know, we
find ourselves one day later at the beginning of proceedings
than General Wyatt states, the night of the selection would be
that of the 8th into the 9th November 1920. On examining
the Fitzsimon documents it was clear that Wyatt, Macdonogh
and Fitzsimon attended the Australian commemoration
ceremony at Amiens Cathedral on the 7th November 1920.
Amiens and St. Pol are some 35 miles apart so it is entirely
plausible that they could have been driven back to St. Pol
later that evening in time for General Wyatt to make the
selection of the body. The attendance of the senior officers
at the Amiens event does not appear out of the ordinary, the
Adjutant General and General Officer Commanding could
easily have delegated the task of coordinating the selection
scheme to a lower ranking officer while they attended the
service. The appearance of Major Fitzsimon however may
raise a question, especially when one considers the statement
made in his curriculum vitae:[9]

> 'Submitted and carried out the scheme for the selection
> of and removal of the remains of the Unknown Warrior
> from the Field to the destroyer Verdun at Boulogne.'

This statement implies that he was there to take part in
or supervise what was *his* scheme and as a middle-ranking
officer in the command structure of the D.G.R.&E. perhaps
he should have been. This point arises of course due to the
difficulty in assembling the timeline of events based on
the letter General Wyatt penned to the *Daily Telegraph* in

---

9 Curriculum Vitae, Ernest S. Fitz-Simon MBE, Fitz-Simon family archive, Dr.
John Fitz-Simon, Canada.

November 1939. This account has been relied upon ever since when journalists and writers attempt to recount the events and invariably results in the authors jumping from the beginning of the story to a point close to the end where the statements that are taken from Wyatt's account can be corroborated by contemporary photographs and news reports as fact. It is as if they had encountered these same difficulties in telling a day by day account as I had.

I spoke again to Dr. John Fitz-Simon, Ernest's son when he came to Belfast on a visit from his home in Canada. John had served as a Medical Doctor in the Royal Army Medical Corps in the rank of Major and could draw on his own military knowledge when recounting what his father, Ernest had told him regarding his military career. I reminded him of the off-the-cuff remark he had made about his father's role in the Unknown Warrior and apologised for taking a rather sceptical view of the comment. I was not alone in taking that initial attitude, I have since discovered that many historians tend to dismiss such information, based on their knowledge of what is an accepted account. Our first hand sources of information for this event are all now long gone, as has our opportunity to question them on what has been documented. John, as Ernest's son was obviously a secondary source but he was nevertheless a very good one as he had specifically spoken to his father about the Unknown Warrior. John gave me three accounts that he had learnt from his father; two, relating to the public 'overt' side of the operation which I had great joy in corroborating, the other, relating to the 'covert' non-public aspect of the selection of the bodies I could not corroborate but have recorded here to allow the reader to add it to the information available as it cannot be proven conclusively nor can it be entirely disregarded.

The first account that John remembered being told by his father related to the French soldiers bringing the body of the Unknown Warrior to the Quayside at Boulogne just prior to it being carried on board H.M.S. *Verdun*. John told me that Ernest had been involved in making the detailed arrangements for the procession from the Citadel at Boulogne to the awaiting H.M.S. *Verdun* moored alongside Quai Chanzy. Ernest had left the Citadel prior to the procession and waited at the dockside with a number of French dignitaries, other British officers and the waiting public and press reporters. John recounts:[10]

> 'H.M.S. *Verdun* – there was quite a row at this point as some French general sent some apparently battered and ancient transport wagon to take the coffin, Fitz [his father] told me that he nearly got him [the general] sacked!'

The problem was that the transport that Fitzsimon had arranged to convey the body had been a gun carriage, instead what had actually arrived for the task was a rather tattered French general service military wagon. John went on to describe how his father had told him he had gone into a rage when he had seen what had happened, contrary to his instructions. A number of photographs in the Fitzsimon archive show scenes at the dockside. Fitzsimon can be clearly seen standing with Marshal Foch and with Generals Wyatt and Macdonogh; the fact that he was there cannot be in doubt. John produced one battered photograph from the collection. It showed the Boulogne Quayside with H.M.S. *Verdun* in the background, the procession in the mid-ground and Marshal Foch standing as if speaking to the crowds in attendance. Behind him stood General Macdonogh. The copy which John produced was very badly damaged. I obtained an identical copy of the original image after discovering it within the Imperial War Museum London collection.[11] Straightaway it could be seen that the coffin containing the Unknown

---

10 Dr. John Fitz-Simon, Personal letter to the author, December 2012.
11 Imperial War Museum Archives, 'The coffin containing the body of the Unknown Warrior on the Quay Chanzy alongside H.M.S. *Verdun* at Boulogne accompanied by French and British Guards of Honour.' Photographs Q 70591.

Warrior, draped with the Union Flag, was indeed carried in a general service wagon, similar, to my untrained eyes, to a farm wagon. It was strange that I had seen photographs of the event before, perhaps even this one, but I had never thought twice about what I was actually looking at. I had also seen photographs showing the Unknown Warrior being carried from the dockside at Dover; there a gun carriage was used. Until I had heard the story I had not been fazed by what I had seen. I then began to examine the high quality version of the image in an attempt to identify others in the photograph. There, on the right side of the image, which was almost a panoramic scene, was Ernest Fitzsimon standing between the procession and the warship in a group of three other British officers and one French officer. I was surprised at what I was looking at. Rather than standing reverently, or even at attention the camera had caught him turned sideways on with his arm extended, he looked to be very angry. Furthermore, the French officer was looking at Fitzsimon and not at the proceedings, as were two of the other British officers in the group. I was seeing the anger that his son had described; interestingly due to the degraded copy of the image that he possessed John had not been aware that his father was in the photograph. I had the pleasure of pointing out to him what I had found. He laughed.

The second remark which, when followed up on, bore fruit, came about while John and I examined the documents relating to his father. From the box of photographs and documents John produced a small white business card. Printed across the card in large lettering was, 'Le Maréshal Foch'. It was the calling card of Ferdinand Foch, the French Supreme Commander during the Great War. I was taken aback by the simplicity of the item. John then informed me that his father had met Marshal Foch just before the operation to repatriate the body of the Unknown Warrior was carried out. I now know that Major Fitzsimon met with Marshal Foch and

General Macdonogh at the service at Amiens Cathedral on the 7th November 1920. At some point during their meeting at Amiens Foch had enquired what the British officers were doing in the coming days. The detail of the Unknown Warrior operation was then outlined. John Fitz-Simon maintained that as a result of the conversation his father had regarding the Unknown Warrior Marshal Foch made a decision to take part in the event to pay his respects to the British warrior, hence his appearance at the quayside at Boulogne. Again, I was aware that Fitz had appeared in a number of photographs alongside Marshal Foch during the two events between the 7th and 10th November 1920. Indeed, the inclusion of the calling card among Fitz's belongings proves to a greater degree that both men had met. How could John's account of the Marshal making the decision to attend the Boulogne quayside event be corroborated? The answer to that question may be found within the National Archive. The file that contained the orders for the Unknown Warrior events contained a communication marked 'secret' and dated the 9th November 1920 from Lord Derby in Paris. It stated:[12]

> 'Marshal Foch and General Weygand are proceeding to Boulogne tonight to do honour to body of unknown British Soldier on its departure from France. I would suggest that His Majesty's Government should send a message of thanks to Marshal Foch who has chosen to do this entirely on his own initiative.'

Further documentation within the file indicate that until that point there had been no planned role for the French authorities at Boulogne. The answer to the question of whether Marshal Foch had been influenced by Fitz can never really be established for certain; the fact remains, Foch did attend the quayside at Boulogne and made the decision to do so just prior to the 9th November.

---

12 The National Archives, Unknown Warrior Orders for UK events, WO 32/3000

The evidence to support the proposition that Major Ernest Fitzsimon was involved in planning and carrying out the scheme regarding the Unknown Warrior was beginning to stack up, but what of the actual planning? What else did his son John know? Over the course of a number of months John focused on his memories of his late father and sent his recollections to me in a series of handwritten letters. He told me of his service after leaving the army in 1921 in the Royal Ulster Constabulary, when he held the rank of Lieutenant Colonel in the C1 Special Constabulary and of his later career as a barrister, the first to practice in both the Northern Ireland and Southern Ireland circuits following partition. John then remembered that he had been told of the selection method employed to select the body of the Unknown Warrior. He wrote of his father:[13]

'I am not clear where the actual method came from, as over the years I've seen a couple of claims (He may have been the author of). Whatever the answer, there is no doubt he organised and ran the whole thing, and was probably the only person with even a vague idea where the body was from, let alone who it was. What was done was France and Belgium were divided into 5 areas. In each area every section picked one unidentified body, then each platoon selected one of those, then company, then battalion, then brigade and so on up to army so finally with 5 bodies for the total war zone. At this point someone came out from Whitehall and together with Fitz, picked one of the five. So Fitz was the only person who knew which zone the body came from, but no more. He then arranged the transport to Boulogne to go to London via H.M.S. *Verdun*.'

John wrote in a later letter, on thinking about what he had written previously; 'It was Wyatt who picked the body.' I had learned through researching soldiers' military history that in

---

13 Dr. John Fitz-Simon, Personal letter to the author, December 2012.

most family accounts that there was usually some part of a family story that was based on fact. There were a number of published articles over the years that touched on the selection aspect of the operation; invariably no two were identical. Again it would have been easy to dismiss this account of the described selection process as I imagined a macabre scene of many bodies moving across each of the army areas for the purpose of the various selection processes from section level all the way to brigade and army level within the D.G.R.&E. When one looks at the information from a distance, there could well be something to it. There is no doubt that some system was required to be put in place to achieve the selection. Maybe rather than physically exhuming bodies for this process it could have been carried out on paper, with each level of D.G.R.&E. command forwarding details of potential unknown battlefield graves identified from each of their respective areas to be selected before the final exhumation work took place.

The question of the number of bodies used for the final selection varies between accounts; again one would expect that from General Wyatt's letter to the *Daily Telegraph* four bodies would be the accepted number. John Fitz-Simon was adamant that the figure was five; indeed I put him over this account on a number of occasions. I studied the account again, it was based on the division of France and Belgium into the five army areas with each area ultimately being responsible for producing one body. I carried out some research into the structure of the British Army in France and Belgium at that time. The British Expeditionary Force (B.E.F.) had fought in France and Flanders with five armies until November 1918; initially the Graves Registration Units were organised to correspond with these five areas of control. Following the Armistice however the Armies, no longer fighting armies as such, reorganised into administrative areas, roughly covering the geographical areas of the former Army footprint. Following this reorganisation the five areas were reduced to four. As if to confuse further these four areas were not numbered simply 1 to 4, there were No.1, No.3, No.4 and No.5 areas but no No.2 area as the Second Army had become the occupying British Army on the Rhine. So although there was a No. 5 Area, there were only four actual administrative areas covering France and Belgium. Therefore, if each area was instructed to produce one body, the total number actually produced would be four, not five.

The next point to address relating to John's account was the number of personnel involved, not so much to carry out the plan as he recounted it but to be in France and Flanders at that time if as described a selection process took place from section level right up to brigade and army level. An account by Lieutenant Colonel Henry Williams, which we shall look at later, describes some 5000 men attached to the D.G.R.&E which he refers to as a 'regiment' at that time involved in graves registration work[14,15], certainly enough to cover the four areas at a strength greater even than a pre-Armistice fighting battalion.

So an account that I have to admit to initially discarding, when looked into with regard to the selection process actually had some legs. There is no doubt that the detail has been lost in the telling as with many second-hand accounts but it can be proven that the source, Major Ernest Fitzsimon, was in a position to have known at least some of what had actually gone on at St. Pol in November 1920. In any case, as far as I could establish there was no account available to state otherwise.

Amongst the Fitzsimon family documents I then came across an official document headed 'British Troops in France and Flanders, Staff Duties, 'Q' Branch'. The officer in charge of the 'Q' Branch, and whose name headed the structure

---

14 *Daily Telegraph*, Obituaries, Lt. Col Henry Williams, 4th October 1993.
15 Imperial War Museum, Oral History, Williams, Henry James Middleton, Catalogue No. 11265, March 1990.

of 'Q' Branch was Staff Officer, Major S.E.S. Fitz-Simon M.B.E., D.A.Q.M.G. (Department of Assistant Quartermaster General). This document listed the responsibilities of the various officers attached to 'Q' Branch. It could be seen straightaway that the unit was sizeable, with officers listed as being in charge of various sub-units, similar to those within a battalion structure, for example Signals, Veterinary, Remounts, Motor Transport, Royal Engineer Companies and so on. Along with this document were a number of group photographs with some headed B. T. In F. and F. (British Troops in France and Flanders) at St. Pol. Straightaway I recognised Generals Wyatt and Macdonogh in the photographs along with the now easily recognisable Major Fitzsimon. Unfortunately none of these images carried any annotation. I decided that if I adopted the same attitude to these documents and photographs as I had to my great-grandfather's notebook there was a chance that I could uncover more information relating to St. Pol and the Unknown Warrior. In other words, if I could identify those named in the 'Q Branch' document and research as many of those names as I could then there was a chance that if they had been involved in the operation in November 1920 then they may have written something or spoke of events to family members. Again, I realised that, to say the least, this course of action was a long shot but at that point I knew who served in 'Q' Branch with Fitzsimon at St. Pol and if they were there then what did they know and what record, if any, did they leave?

HARDWICKE

During a later telephone call with John Fitz-Simon he made another off-the-cuff remark about his father having been the last British Expeditionary Force (B.E.F.) soldier to leave France. This comment was followed up a few weeks later with a copy of the *Daily Mirror* arriving in the post from Canada. The newspaper edition was dated October 28th 1921; it was an original copy and on page 8 there was a story and two photographs beneath a heading 'Last of the B.E.F. in France'. The first photograph showed a group of four soldiers named as Major E.S. Fitzsimon, Lieutenant C.W. Hardwicke, CSM Pratt and Lance Corporal Parker. The four men were posed with a German Mercedes staff car; a second photograph was of a little terrier dog called Old Bill who it was reported had gone to France with the Army Service Corps in 1914 and was 'The last to leave'. I recognised the name 'C.W. Hardwicke' from the 'Q Branch' list; a Lieutenant working in the office of the St. Pol Camp Commandant Captain A.W. Smith O.B.E. I then found an identical photograph to that which was published in the *Daily Mirror* within the Fitzsimon collection. With this photograph I was able to identify Lieutenant Cedric Hardwicke amongst the officers in the main St. Pol group photograph along with Fitzsimon, Wyatt and Macdonogh.

Cedric Webster Hardwicke had been an actor when the war first started. He obtained a commission from the Inns of Court Officer Training Corps into the Royal Army Service Corps, 34th Division, and was deployed to France in January 1916. He later served with the Northumberland Fusiliers in early 1918. In November 1918 he was granted home leave, the last day of which coincided with Armistice Day. The following day he requested an extension to his 'temporary' commission whereupon he was sent to General Headquarters at St. Pol. Later, in his autobiography '*Let's Pretend*', written in 1932, he briefly describes some of his time at St. Pol alongside a photograph identical to that in the *Daily Mirror* and Fitzsimon collection showing the 'Last B.E.F. soldiers to leave'. He wrote:[16]

'I had the strange distinction of being, officially, the last British officer to leave the war zone – hardly, however, such a distinction as being the first one to reach it. My

---

16 '*Let's Pretend, Recollections and Reflections of a Lucky Actor*', Cedric Hardwicke, Grayson & Grayson Ltd. London 1932.

final duty was to haul down the Union Jack which had contrived to flutter over G.H.Q. since the days when Haig was in command. That flag still reposes in my old theatre basket, in company with many relics of war concert parties.'

Hardwicke goes on to tell the story of the little terrier 'Old Bill'.

'In the camp was a little fox-terrier known as Old Bill who had come over to France with the first Expeditionary Force. Everybody had loved Old Bill, for he was a real soldier, and he had loved everybody in return. To my dismay I discovered that the quarantine restrictions would prevent me from taking him back to England, and I felt heartbroken at the thought of having to leave him in St. Pol with the French, who naturally would have little sentiment for him. Eventually I wrote to an Englishman in Paris whom I had known slightly, explaining the position and he at once agreed to have the dog. He met Old Bill at the station and took him home to the suburbs; but Bill hated civilian life, and a few days later was found lying dead at the station. I shall always think that he found his way there hoping to rejoin his old friends the tommies, and, finding the station full of unimportant civilians, died of disappointment.'

The heartbreaking story of Old Bill explains the presence of the dog in the photograph; the tattered flag Hardwicke describes which flew over the headquarters at St. Pol can be found today in the Somme Heritage Centre in County Down, Northern Ireland.

When it comes to the story of the Unknown Warrior however Cedric Hardwicke gives a brief but very significant account of the role he played in the operation:[17]

'It was at St. Pol that the body of the Unknown Warrior was selected. It devolved upon me to hoodwink the

17 Ibid.

special newspaper correspondents who came from England to find out "all about it". I hope these gentlemen have long since forgiven me the wild goose chases I sent them to far-away villages whenever any decisive step was being taken. I never walk past the Cenotaph without recollecting the night when I mounted guard with other officers over the body of the Unknown Warrior until dawn, in the makeshift chapel of St. Pol. It was an unforgettable experience.'

This paragraph, although brief, highlights two important points which will become relevant later. Firstly it is obvious that there was in place at the time a deliberate strategy with regard to the press, whereby misinformation was disseminated to detract from the covert aspect of the Unknown Warrior operation. This takes us some way towards differences in accounts that appeared after the event. Secondly, Lieutenant Hardwicke was allocated the task of guarding the body overnight at St. Pol following the selection of the body. In General Wyatt's 1939 account he describes 'passing the guard which had been specially mounted.' The significance of this we will come to later but it shows us that there was a deliberate decision to allocate the tasks surrounding the selection process to officers, rather than to 'other ranks'. Lieutenant Hardwicke was a relatively low ranking officer within the command structure at St. Pol but still would normally have been above the task of guarding a body overnight when there were non commissioned officers and lower ranking soldiers available to adequately carry out such a task.

Cedric Hardwicke returned to his acting career following seven years of military service. He went on to have a very successful career in both theatre and moving pictures. He was knighted in 1934, at that time the youngest actor to receive such an accolade. He married twice. His first wife actress Helena Pickard was the sister of Royal Air Force Group Captain Percy Pickard who was killed in action leading the daring low-level bombing raid 'Operation Jericho' on Amiens Prison in France in February 1944. Cedric Hardwicke's second marriage was to American actress Mary Scott. Sir Cedric Hardwicke passed away on the 6th August 1964 at the age of 71.

BRODIE

I returned once more to the 'Q' Branch document. Above Lieutenant Hardwicke's name was typed the name of the Camp Commandant, Captain A.W. Smith O.B.E. This name appeared on two additional documents, a photograph and a letter. The photograph showed him being awarded a medal, possibly his O.B.E., by General Wyatt. In the background can be seen Major Fitzsimon and a lady identified as General Wyatt's wife. The letter, signed by A.W. Smith, was written on Royal Army Service Corps headed paper, from Buller Barracks, Aldershot, addressed 'Dear Fitz' and dated 13th October 1921.[18] In the text of the letter Captain Smith asks of a number of people he had served with; in one sentence he made reference to a surname, '*I am going to see The Brodie some day soon, probably Sunday.*' The name 'Brodie' rang a bell. I had studied the National Army Museum archive and had found two letters written by a lady who had served with the Queen Mary's Women's Army Auxiliary Corps, (Q.M.W.A.A.C.) and had been attached to the D.G.R.&E. at St. Pol. This lady was called Margaret Vere Brodie of Brodie, Scotland. Three women featured in the group photograph of the staff at St. Pol. One of these ladies, wearing a Q.M.W.A.A.C. officer's uniform, could be seen to be wearing the three Great War service medal ribbons indicating that she had been awarded the British War, Victory and 1914/15 Star medals. I checked the medal rolls for these medals under the name Brodie and confirmed that Margaret V. Brodie of Brodie had served in France from April 1915 as a volunteer nurse. This indicated

18 Fitz-Simon Family Archive, Dr. John Fitz-Simon, Canada.

that she had been qualified to wear all three medal ribbons by 1921 when the group photograph had been taken. I then enquired with the Scottish National Trust archives at Brodie Castle in Nairn, the seat of the Brodie Clan. Photographs from the archives at Brodie Castle confirmed that the lady in the St. Pol group photograph was in fact Margaret Vere Brodie. Two signed personal accounts which outline her military service initially as a Voluntary Aid Detachment (V.A.D.) nurse and later, from 1917 on, as a member of the Q.M.W.A.A.C. serving after the Armistice as part of the Army of Occupation in Germany, were held at the National Army Museum in London. Vere Brodie ended her military service at St. Pol where she held the rank of Senior Unit Administrator in charge of 31 other Q.M.W.A.A.C. ladies attached to the D.G.R.&E. In each of her accounts she makes reference to the Unknown Warrior, proving one questionable point and unfortunately clouding over another.

In her first record of her service at St. Pol she describes an account of the selection of the body of the Unknown Warrior:[19]

'From our camp went out the body of the Unknown Warrior. On the night of November 8 1920, three remains of unknown soldiers were brought in separately by ambulance from three different battle areas and laid in our small camp chapel. The G.O.C. General Wyatt, went to the chapel, chose one of the remains and placed him in a simple wooden coffin, and guards were posted. Very few people knew what was going on, but the next morning a notice was put up saying: "The Camp Chapel will be open from 10.30 to 11.30 hours in order that all ranks who wish to do so may view the coffin containing the remains of The Unknown British Warrior." The hushed thrill in the camp all that day was marvellous. The

---

19 National Army Museum Collection, Memoirs of Vere Brodie Entitled 'Tea and Talk' NAM.1998-01-26-2

Unknown Warrior was taken to Boulogne in an Army ambulance with a bodyguard of eight Sergeants. There the French Army took over until next morning, when the Unknown Warrior in a magnificent coffin sent out from London, was taken over by an escort of the Royal Navy. The beginning, so simple and sincere, was wonderful.'

Vere Brodie's recollection, when we look at it from the perspective of the event timeline gives us a sound sequence of events, importantly beginning on the night of the 8th November 1920. The further events which she described over the subsequent days fit with what we know as fact. Based on this account, which is of a more contemporaneous nature than General Wyatt's 1939 letter, and on the difficulties encountered in beginning the story on the 7th November 1920, I would tend to accept the 8th as being the start date and the night on which the bodies were selected. This brings us to Vere Brodie's point on the number of bodies selected being three. On reading through her account again she makes one quite telling comment: '*Very few people knew what was going on.*' When we take that comment into consideration and reread through the extract, it appears that her actual consciousness of the events she described began the following morning with her description of the sign at the chapel and perhaps with the guard having been posted but, either way, subsequent to the selection process having already taken place. When we consider this it seems that she may not have had any knowledge of events, or numbers of bodies for that matter, prior to the guard being mounted at the chapel. Nevertheless she recalled that the number three was significant in relation to the selection process.

In Vere's second account she provides us with an account of her, and the other Q.M.W.A.A.C ladies, leaving France on the 26th September 1921. I had discovered that Major Ernest Fitzsimon and Lieutenant Cedric Hardwicke were the last B.E.F. men to leave France and now had found one of the last women to leave, just four weeks before the men. In actual fact Vere Brodie had certainly served in a 'Theatre of War' for much longer than either Fitzsimon or Hardwicke. Brodie described her journey back to London from France with more than an element of pride and emotion in being, as she described a 'Last Waac'. Indeed, rather than disperse and disappear back into civilian life her unit had one very important task to complete while they were still together in London:[20]

'We finally demobilised at The War Office and visited the Command Paymaster Office next day, 27th September 1921. That was the official end, but the members unanimously felt that they would, as their last act, like to take some flowers to the Cenotaph. So, at 10 a.m. on the 28th, as many as were able, all had subscribed, met in Whitehall, and we laid our wreath at the foot of the Cenotaph to the "Boys" who, unlike ourselves, would not come back. We then went to Westminster Abbey to visit the grave of the Unknown Warrior. We, from St. Pol, have a special feeling towards the Unknown Warrior, as it was in our camp chapel that he lay the night of the 8th-9th November 1920, before being carried to Boulogne and England, and Westminster Abbey. I would like, on behalf of the last unit, to thank all the ex-Waac's who came to Victoria Station, and who gave us such a splendid welcome on our return. It was very much appreciated, and made us realise fully that we were not 31 Waacs, but members of a great army. I think we all felt very proud of ourselves in consequence.'

In telling her story of remembrance Vere once again makes mention of the 8th-9th November 1921 selection date. The fact that she led an act of remembrance at the Cenotaph and then at the grave of the Unknown Warrior is not at all

---

20 National Army Museum Collection, Memoirs of Vere Brodie Queen Mary's Army Auxiliary Corps 1921. NAM.1998-01-26-1

surprising. Vere had lost a brother and a cousin in the Great War. Both men had served in the 1st Battalion of The Cameron Highlanders. Her brother Captain Douglas Edward Brodie was killed in action on the 19th August 1916 during one of a series of attacks mounted to attempt to take High Wood, north-west of Longueval, in the Somme region of France. High Wood was a strategic position held by the Germans during the Battle of the Somme; it was the last of a series of woods in the general area taken as a result of gruesome fighting during the Somme offensive that included Mametz Wood, Delville Wood and Trones Wood. British efforts to take the wood began on the 14th July 1916 during what became known as the Battle for Bazentin Ridge. After a series of attacks mounted over several weeks High Wood finally fell on the 15th September 1916 at a terrible overall cost to life. Captain Douglas Brodie was initially buried east of the little village of Bazentin-le-Petit. His grave was later exhumed after the Armistice with some 5,500 others, recovered from small battlefield cemeteries and individual graves around the area, and reburied in the nearby Caterpillar Valley Cemetery. On the 6th November 2004 the remains of an unknown New Zealand soldier were exhumed from this cemetery and laid to rest in Wellington, New Zealand, representing that nation's Unknown Warrior.

Vere Brodie's cousin, Captain Ewan James Brodie of Lethen had deployed to France and Flanders at the outbreak of the war on the 21st August 1914, a year or so before Douglas. Captain Ewan Brodie was killed in action at Glencourse Wood near Westhoek in Belgium during the First Battle of Ypres. Hi body was recovered at the time and buried close to where he fell. His grave was lost during subsequent fighting, the location however had been recorded and in 1923 the Brodie family purchased a plot of land in the area where the grave was indicated to have been. A private memorial was erected which remains there to this day. On it is carved;

'To the glory of God and in memory of Ewan James Brodie, Captain 1st Batt. Queen's Own Cameron Highlanders who was killed at the first battle of Ypres 11th Nov 1914. Buried near this spot.'

Captain Ewan Brodie is officially remembered by the Commonwealth War Graves Commission on the Menin Gate Memorial to the Missing in Ypres along with the names of over 55,000 other soldiers who were killed and have no known grave.

It is therefore of no surprise that Vere Brodie organised the very personal act of remembrance at the Cenotaph and Westminster Abbey on returning to London in September 1921 for she had suffered the same loss as the many thousands of bereaved who had passed by the grave of the Unknown Warrior the previous year. For her, the first simple act of remembrance in filing past the body of the Unknown Warrior at St. Pol held particular personal significance. Vere Brodie was obviously a remarkable lady. From our 21st-century viewpoint it is impossible to imagine the stresses over protracted periods that people like her, and the others mentioned in this book, were functioning under; ordinary people, grasped from a normal life and thrust into the nightmare that was the Great War when extraordinary feats were expected from them. Vere's recollection of the moment the war ended on the 11th November 1918, also by cruel coincidence the fourth anniversary of Ewan Brodie's death, is short but telling:

'I was in this camp on the morning of Armistice Day and happened to be alone in my office at 11 o'clock and heard the hooters of the ships at Avonmouth announcing the news that peace had come. Like thousands of others, I broke down completely and cried as I had not cried all through those anxious and sad years. Luckily no one saw me.'

Vere Brodie's solemn and respectful act of remembrance at Westminster Abbey had been mirrored by hundreds of thousands of people during the preceding months since

November 1920. In the years following, as much as the people accepted the grave of the Unknown Warrior as a point of mourning for their individual grief and quietly accepted or were indifferent to the secret nature of the selection process involved in choosing him, the story contained that level of intrigue that an enquiring mind just cannot let go of. The brilliance of the plan was the fact that nobody could or should ever know where the body came from, if the integrity of the operation remained intact so too did the all-inclusive point of national remembrance. If even one aspect of the plan was divulged the whole concept of an Unknown Warrior would be destroyed in the minds of the public. Most military secret operations remain just that, secret. This operation crossed the line being secret and covert in preparation to becoming very public and overt over the course of just a few days and before the body even left France the press were speculating on the details. A *Times* report dated midday on the 10th November 1920 and published on the 11th carried the story 'Marshal Foch's Farewell'; in the third paragraph the special correspondent reported:[21]

'As the sun was sinking yesterday afternoon, an Army ambulance arrived at Boulogne from St. Pol with the body, which had been brought "from the Ypres front".

Such a comment could have caused additional pain to those bereaved whose loved ones had disappeared fighting in a region, nowhere near 'the Ypres front'. This point was quickly picked up on at the time by Lieutenant Colonel J. Bradstock, Deputy Director of the D.G.R.&E. and a memo was despatched by him to the Adjutant General's office on the 13th November 1920 addressing this point:[22]

'There are various statements appearing in the press regarding the locality from where the "Unknown

---

21 *The Times*, 'Marshal Foch's Farewell, 11th November 1920.
22 Commonwealth War Graves Commission Archive file No. ADD 6/1/16, 1/11/1920–22/10/2009

Warrior" came. The "Times" I believe state definitely that he came from Ypres, and so on.

Would it not be well to publish an authoritative statement to the effect that the matter was so arranged that this "Unknown Warrior" may have come from anywhere on the Battle Front from the Yser to the Aisne, but that no body, not even the General, knows from where, so that any statement that he came from <u>any</u> particular front must be untrue.

We took enormous trouble to make certain of this, and I think it would perhaps be a good thing to publish this.

You can say with absolute certainty that no one in this world knows where he came from. All we know is that he is an unknown British soldier who was killed fighting our war.'

No official rebuttal or explanation was printed at that time; the Unknown Warrior remained unknown. Occasionally newspaper accounts surfaced from officers declaring that they knew part of or planned the operation. The names of some of these officers appear in the 'Q' Branch document and some of them have been identified in the group photograph of those officers at St. Pol in 1920. Their appearance in the photograph and staff list is undeniable and adds weight to the accounts that they later produce but when it comes to explaining the selection procedure these accounts all differ. I have no doubt that these men were involved to some extent in the operation, and were perhaps not even aware of the fact at the time; for a secret operation to be successful no one person should know the complete plan.

Accounts of the operation did not however go unnoticed. On the 8th November 1923 the Toronto 'Star' carried a story under the banner 'Officer who selected unknown soldier here'. The story began:[23]

---

23 *The Star*, Toronto, 'Officer Who Selected Unknown Warrior Here.' 8th November 1923.

'The officer to whom was committed the task of locating and bringing to London, England the body of the Unknown Soldier, is now a resident in Toronto. He is Captain J.J. Walsh, of the Connaught Rifles, and one of the staff of the Imperial War Graves Commission.'

Straight away a couple of inconsistencies with the reported narrative can be seen. The use of the term 'Unknown Soldier' contrary to the inclusive 'warrior' that was decided upon and the inclusion of the 'Imperial War Graves Commission' as the unit responsible raise a question. The regiment in which Captain Walsh purportedly served, The Connaught Rifles did not exist. The Connaught Rangers fought during the Great War as did the Royal Irish Rifles but not a combination of these two names. This extract of the report could be put down to poor journalism on behalf of the reporter. Captain Walsh is then quoted directly in the report:

'After receiving instructions I took twelve men with me and went out to one of the battlefields of Flanders. We began our search. We were able to tell from the colour of the soil where a body might be found. Several were dug up until we came across one that was absolutely without marks or identification. There was no disc, no number or sign on the clothing of anything whatever to show who it might be.

All that I can say is that the body was clothed in a Private's uniform but that is not even significant for many officers when they went into action often used the uniform of a Private soldier. The body was stripped of its clothing, wrapped in a canvas, then placed in a coffin...'

If the account had stopped at that point in Captain Walsh's quote it could be entirely believable, if somewhat uninteresting. We know from the instructions from the Adjutant General in October 1920 that the exhumed body had to be unidentifiable. Captain Walsh mentioned Flanders as the location of the exhumation he described; this of course excluded the possibility of a body having come from any of the other battlefields. If Captain Walsh had been ordered to do just as he had stated thus far in his account and had been told nothing else the statement is a plausible one. He may well have been part of the operation, providing one of the bodies for selection, unaware of what else was taking place elsewhere that day or what took place at St. Pol later. Unfortunately four more words are included in his quote,

> '...and shipped to London.' He adds, 'That is all that can be known or is known about the identity of the unknown soldier.'

The report went on to repeat that Captain Walsh had served with the Connaught Rifles before service with the Imperial War Graves Commission (I.W.G.C.) in 1919. Maybe it was the case that the reporter misquoted Walsh or had 'gilded the lily' slightly to add interest to the story. In any case the report was brought to the attention of none other than Fabian-Ware who forwarded it to General Macdonogh for comment, whose reply, held in the Commonwealth War Graves Commission archive, was scathing:

> '8th Jan 1924. My dear Ware, Captain Walsh is an unmitigated liar. As you know the I.W.G.C. had nothing to do with the Unknown Warrior, he was selected by the D.G.R.&E. at St. Pol. The story that only one body was disinterred, somewhere in Flanders and brought from there to London is untrue. So is Walsh's statement that he accompanied the body to London. The only people who did were Wyatt and myself.
>
> It was decided at the time that we should not publish the facts regarding the selection of the body and I don't think it would be possible to enter into a press controversy with Walsh without going against that decision. My advice would be to leave it alone. If the British press were to take it up we could reconsider it.'

The official policy therefore was to not confirm nor deny.

Prior to General Wyatt's definitive account published in the *Daily Telegraph* on the 11th November 1939 a number of accounts had surfaced stating differences in the numbers of bodies involved in the selection. One such account by the Reverend George Kendall O.B.E., a chaplain based at St. Pol at the time, was published in the *Daily Herald* on the 17th May 1930. In this account Reverend Kendall is quoted to have stated when asked about the number of bodies involved:

> 'We took one from an unknown grave in the Ypres salient, and others from the Marne, the Arras and the Cambrai fronts. A sixth came from a grave much further south. All the six, identical in appearance, were placed in a hut and the door was locked. Next morning, a general Officer entered the hut alone and chose one of the coffins. The five other bodies were given a proper burial.'

The report continues with the Reverend Kendall quoted as adding:

> 'I walked in the procession through Boulogne with the bodies of the six heroes' and 'The six bodies were placed in a hut and the door was locked. Later the General Officer commanding the troops entered the hut alone and selected a body.'

On 9th November 1938 a letter was published in the *Daily Telegraph* which had been sent to the editor, signed E. E. Laws. Laws stated that he had been attached to St. Pol at the time of the Unknown Warrior selection and, although he repeated the six body narrative, wrote that the selection took place on the night of the 8th or first hours of the 9th November 1920:[24]

> 'The British Empire's Unknown was chosen either very late on the night of Nov. 8 or in the first hours of Nov. 9, 1920. Six flag-shrouded bodies were placed in the Roman Catholic chapel-hut at St. Pol, Pas-de-Calais'.

---

24 *Daily Telegraph* 'Symbol of the Unknown Warrior' E.E. Laws, 11th November 1938.

This part of his account was not however written as a witness to the events; he writes first hand:[25]

> 'It may console many millions of His Majesty's Roman Catholic subjects that on the morning of Nov. 9, 1920, while the Unknown was still in the chapel-hut at St. Pol, Pas-De-Calais, I as Roman Catholic chaplain, celebrated in that hut a requiem mass for the world's war dead, irrespective of nationality, and, in case the body was that of a Catholic, I performed over it the ceremony of absolution.'

Again, by the nature of his account he could very well have conducted the mass with the body on the morning of the 9th November but his account of the number of bodies selected has to be looked upon as hearsay.

With all of these conflicting and partial accounts entering the public domain it is of no surprise that General Wyatt broke ranks to put the records straight in November 1939. He was, after all, the officer in charge of the operation, even if, as it appears, it was planned in such a way that even he could not have known all of the details of its conception. If Major Ernest Fitzsimon's simple statement in his 1942 curriculum vitae informing the reader that he planned and carried out this scheme was to be believed, one thing was certain, he did not tell the press, the only person he did tell, many years later, was his son John. Significantly, his account of the method of selection appears nowhere else in the many published accounts over the past century. Fitzsimon's plan was secret. As an officer with strong military intelligence pedigree one thing was certain; he knew how to keep a secret, especially when the consequences of not doing so meant loss of life, or, in the case of this operation, loss of hope for millions of people.

---

25 Ibid.

CECIL MILLER SMITH

Subsequent to November 1939 writers re-telling the story of the Unknown Warrior tended to default to General Wyatt's *Daily Telegraph* account and struggled through the 7th November timeline date issue. Some however attempted to add parts of previously published accounts in an attempt to exercise due diligence to their reporting. Such an example was published in the 1st November 1967 edition of the Australian *Reveille* magazine by E.C. Sier. In this account six bodies were brought for selection which took place at midnight on November 9th–10th. The next day the Reverend Kendall escorted one body from St. Pol to Boulogne. Interestingly this account makes reference to Fitzsimon:[26]

> '...the ambulance drew up at the ancient castle, the local headquarters of the French Army. Here to meet it were Colonel Bradstock, Colonel Gell, Major Fitzsimons [spelt with an 's'.], Major Diebold of the French Army and M. Labeau, Sub-Prefect of the district.'

As those officers who were of senior rank back in 1920 began to pass away the task of keeping the story on an even keel fell to those men who were of relatively junior rank when the operation was carried out; lieutenants and captains. One such officer was Cecil Miller Smith. Cecil Smith was born in June 1896 at Dromore, County Down in Northern Ireland. He attended Belfast Royal Academical Institute (R.B.A.I.) from 1909 until 1914 when he was admitted to the Royal Military Academy at Sandhurst. He served in the Great War in the Royal Army Service Corps and The Royal Inniskilling Fusiliers and was awarded the Military Cross. As a professional soldier he remained in the Army after 1919 when he was attached to the D.G.R.&E. in which he served as both Lieutenant and Captain rank. Between the wars he studied engineering while serving with the Royal

---

26 *Reveille* magazine, 'How They Chose The Unknown Warrior'. E.C. Sier, 1st November 1967.

Army Service Corps as a matriculated student of Queen's University in Belfast. He made use of his engineering skills overseas in Shanghai and India while deployed on various military and civilian engineering projects, specialising in the construction of heavy repair facilities. In 1934 he became a member of the Institution of Mechanical Engineers. During the 1939 to 1945 war he distinguished himself in the North African Campaign in his organisation of Field Maintenance Areas in the Western Desert leading up to the German defeat at El Alamein. Between 1943 and 1945 he served as deputy Assistant Chief of Staff, Supreme Headquarters of the Allied Expeditionary Force in Europe. Smith received a Knighthood in 1947 and retired from the Army in 1951 after which he took up an honorary post as Colonel Commandant of the Royal Army Service Corps and chaired the Royal Ulster Society in London between 1964 and 1973.

Cecil Miller Smith appears on the Headquarters 'Q Branch' document as Staff Captain reporting to Major Ernest Fitzsimon. He was photographed along with Fitzsimon and Cedric Hardwicke and can also be seen standing beside Fitz in a photograph dated 26th October 1920 titled 'Hockey Match, Ireland v The Rest of the World' wearing a large shamrock badge on his jersey as a member of the Ireland team. Smith also appeared in the St. Pol group photo along with Vere Brodie, Fitz, Cedric Hardwicke, Wyatt and Macdonogh. With his appearance in both the Hockey Team photograph and the larger group photograph we can say that he was at St. Pol across the relevant time period between the 7th and 11th November 1920, when the Unknown Warrior operation took place. Any account of the event that he made must hold some weight. On the 15th November 1980, sixty years after the event, the Very Reverend Neil Collings, Chaplain of Westminster for five years prior, wrote an account of the Unknown Warrior story which was published in the *Times* newspaper. The account followed closely the narrative of General Wyatt, mentioning the four bodies and the selection taking place on the night of the 7th November 1920. Reverend Collings encountered the now familiar gap in the timeline that comes with beginning the story on the 7th but finished seamlessly with the body being laid to rest in Westminster Abbey. During the account he repeated the section from Wyatt's 1939 account:

> 'Brigadier-General Wyatt selected one of the bodies and he and the colonel [Gell] placed it in the shell. The lid was screwed down. The other bodies were removed and reburied in the military cemetery at St. Pol.'

This section of the account told nothing revelatory, nor did it veer from General Wyatt's accepted version of events. Neil Collings however sparked an immediate reply from the then Major General Sir Cecil Smith. On the same date Sir Cecil Smith replied:[27]

> 'Dear Padre, I have read with interest your excellent article in todays "Times" entitled "The Inspiration Behind the Unknown Warrior."
>
> I notice however that you inadvertently perpetuate an error which has occurred in other accounts, about the disposal of the three surplus bodies, in stating that they were buried in the Military cemetery at St. Pol.
>
> This is incorrect.
>
> You will appreciate that recent disposal of the three unknown but unselected soldiers was of importance. The sudden appearance of three unknown graves in St. Pol-Sur-Ternoise Military Cemetery, which was a cemetery of a military hospital (by that time closed), where all the dead were probably known, might have caused undesirable speculation.
>
> What actually happened was as follows. At midnight, when the selected body had been removed I drove

---

27 Major-General Sir Cecil Smith letter to Revd. Collings 15th November 1980, Westminster Abbey Muniment 63774B

an ambulance to the hut where the three bodies lay. I was accompanied by a Lieut. Col. and a Major of the Graves Registration Service and by a Chaplain [the Revd, George Standing who afterwards became Deputy Chaplain General of the Army]. We placed the bodies in the ambulance and I drove through the night to a previously reconnoitred and carefully map referenced spot on the Albert–Bapaume Road. On arrival the bodies were placed in an old trench which was filled in. The Padre held a short service. Later it was checked from G.R.E. burial records that the remains of three unknown soldiers had been recovered at the map reference where we had left them and had of course been buried under that description: No connection with the three surplus bodies at St. Pol was suspected. I am writing this because I think you may be interested and I have no intention of writing to the editor of the 'Times'. It is odd that no one seems to have taken the trouble to check at the St. Pol cemetery where of course the graves of three unknown soldiers are likely to be found. The proceedings of that cold frosty night from the picking up of the bodies in camp to their disposal were not so simple as the above may sound.

I will elaborate on this for your benefit should you so wish – not for publication!

George Standing is long since dead and so, I imagine are the other two. I was the youngest and am now 84!'

This was a remarkable letter for a number of reasons, not least the fact that we now have someone who was prepared and qualified to state that General Wyatt had been mistaken in part of his account and that this mistake had been perpetuated over again through the passage of years. The problem was that the mistake was not that of the date, or the number of bodies brought for selection, but the burial of the bodies that were not selected. When one reads the general account of the

Unknown Warrior one is filled with a sense that this was a brilliant idea, well-executed, fulfilling the brief of providing a point of mourning for the nation. But always at the back of my mind at any rate was the question, what happened to the unselected bodies? I have to admit to being one of the people to whom Sir Cecil Smith referred to when he indicated that no one had seemed to have taken the trouble to check the cemetery at St. Pol. I personally checked the cemetery at St. Pol a number of years ago, chasing the story of the Unknown Warrior and can confirm that the general was correct, there are not three unknown burials there. I looked again at General Wyatt's account; he stated that the body selected was placed in the coffin by him and with the help of Colonel Gell he screwed down the lid. He went on to say that the three remaining bodies were removed and buried at the cemetery outside his headquarters at St. Pol but he didn't state that he actually saw that happen or was present when it did. Did his role in the selection part of the plan end once the body was placed in the coffin? He may have believed that the three remaining bodies were buried at St. Pol but he doesn't provide us with evidence in his account to prove that this is what actually happened.

So what of the other points raised in Sir Cecil Smith's letter? An interesting observation is that, as far as we can ascertain from the accounts to hand the work on the operation was carried out by officers only. Cedrick Hardwicke, a Lieutenant at the time, mounted guard overnight; Cecil Smith, also of Lieutenant rank, stated that he drove the three bodies to the specified burial point in an Army ambulance along with a Lieutenant Colonel, a Major and the Chaplain, Reverend Standing. General Wyatt and Colonel Gell carried and placed the selected body into the coffin. There was no mention of any of the lesser tasks being left for 'other ranks' to carry out. The integrity of the covert aspect could be maintained by officers, with regard to anyone else; a need to know policy applied.

The notion of the leaving of the bodies to be recovered again at the specified grid reference along the Albert–Bapaume Road raised more questions. What if they were not recovered as planned? Although a location was carefully reconnoitred and the map reference recorded in Smith's account this information was not to assist in the body recovery, it was to be used to trawl Graves Registration Unit (G.R.U.) returns to check if three bodies had been found at that location. What if three other unconnected bodies were found and the originals missed? The original men were of course unidentifiable. Or what if the original three bodies were missed altogether? On the 'Q Branch' structure it can be seen that the D.G.R.&E. Headquarters Unit at St. Pol had a Royal Army Ordnance Corps unit attached to it, commanded by Ordnance Officer, Major H. Wheeler MC. Unexploded ordnance, a problem for local farmers today, was most definitely a hazard to the G.R.U. recovery teams in 1920. If an unexploded shell had been discovered in the area prior to the bodies being found a controlled Ordnance Corps detonation could scatter the remains to dust. There are many reasons why the bodies might not be found, so why leave that aspect of an otherwise sound and well planned operation to chance?

On the 9th November 2008 a comprehensive account of the Unknown Warrior story was published in the *Daily Telegraph* online edition. It followed the accepted General Wyatt account in that the 7th November date was included as the start date. Other details were included in the account that had not appeared in the 1939 story; for instance a mention was made of the coffin used and of the differing accounts that stated six bodies were brought for selection. The last two sentences of the report describe a rather cold and disturbing sequence of events describing the disposal of the three remaining bodies:[28]

---

28 *Daily Telegraph* on-line edition, 9th November 2008. https://www.telegraph.co.uk/news/uknews/defence/3399166/The-Unknown-Warrior-A-heros-return.html, accessed on 8/3/2020.

'Amid all the public anguish, no one thought to wonder what had become of the other three bodies that had been disinterred from their unmarked graves. A rather less exalted fate awaited them.

After Brig. Wyatt had made his choice, the Union flags were folded away. Then the three bodies were loaded onto the back of a truck, tipped into a shell hole beside the road near the town of Albert and promptly forgotten.'

I found it difficult to accept that the three bodies were disposed of like rubbish by men who had served through the horrors of the war and had witnessed their own friends and colleagues being blown to nothing and lost forever. The Unknown Warrior was as important to the men and women of the D.G.R.&E. as it was to the families and loved ones back in Britain. The purpose of the D.G.R.&E. was to recover and if possible identify remains of soldiers and to afford them a proper burial, whether identified or not.

Sir Cecil Smith alluded to a further account where he would elaborate for the benefit of Reverend Collings. This was forthcoming and is included with the original letter in the Westminster Abbey archives. The letter tells a remarkable story, describing events on the night and early morning of the selection of the body in incredible detail. The start date however reverts back to the 7th/8th November date as outlined by General Wyatt, the remainder of the content is amazing:[29]

'Disposal of the three bodies not selected as the Unknown Warrior

Maj. Gen Sir Cecil Smith.

Presumably it was thought that the sudden appearance of three unknown British soldier graves in St. Pol- Sur- Ternoise Military Cemetery might appear a little odd, particularly as that cemetery, having been filled from a

29 Major-General Sir Cecil Smith letter to Revd. Collings, November 1980, Westminster Abbey Muniment 63774B

military hospital probably had no other "unknown" graves. The plan as related below was therefore brought into effect. Reconnaisance was carried out, personally by a Lt. Col. (name not recollected) of the Graves Registration Service and Major Williams of that service in an area [inserted: in the devastated area] some distance N.W. along the Albert–Bapaume Road which was known to be under active search. You will appreciate that the search for bodies was going on continuously along a settled plan.

The idea was that the bodies should be deposited under earth cover in the area where they would be found by the searchers and re-interred as Unknown British Soldiers. I was detailed to draw an ambulance car from workshops. I duly did so making sure that the vehicle, a Daimler, which I had assumed had been recently overhauled was complete with oil, petrol, water, spare wheel, tool kit and so on.

At midnight 7th/8th Nov I took the vehicle to the hut where the three bodies then lay. You will appreciate that by November 1920 the majority of the bodies of soldiers buried were little more than skeletons with perhaps a few rags of clothing. This applied particularly to unknown bodies, many of which had probably been blown to pieces in the first instance and none of which, including the Unknown Warrior and his companions would be more than a bag (sand bag) full of the approximate bones, including a skull to make up a complete body. As we were not going to dispose of the temporary coffins in which they had been brought in from the areas, we had little of substance to carry.

The "crew" of our vehicle (an ambulance had been selected as appropriate but an ordinary touring car would have sufficed) consisted of 2nd Class Chaplain to the Forces the Rev. George Standing, the Lt. Col. mentioned above, Major Williams and myself, (at that time Lieut.

C.M. Smith MC, R.A.S.C.) assembled at the church. As driver I took no part in handling the bodies but these were placed in the back of the vehicle on one side, the three live passengers occupying the other side. No one volunteered to ride in front with me! It was a bright frosty moonlit night: An ambulance in those days had no windscreen and no door to the driver's seat. It had a canvas apron and two canvas sheets where one would now find doors. Very draughty indeed.

Off we went, it was shortly after midnight and it was mentioned that, all being well we would reach our destination about 4am. But all did not go entirely well. I stopped once to run up and down the road to get warm, my living passengers were all right, they had blankets and they had a flask of rum! They sang hymns – well not always hymns.

Then there began an ominous popping in the carburettor. It got worse. It could only be one thing: water in the petrol, not an unusual happening as stocks of Army petrol were used up. There was only one cure, take off the top of the carburettor float chamber, remove the float, mop up the petrol/water mixture with a rag, (having turned off the petrol) and turn the petrol on again in the hope that there would be no more water. I had a flash lamp and the necessary tools but I found that, in this engine, the float chamber was under the inlet manifold and a nut had to be slackened to allow the carburettor to swing out from under the manifold as there was not room otherwise to lift the cover. But the nut was seized and all my efforts could not move it.

So on we had to go at a much reduced speed and sounding like a machine gun. We reached our destination about two hours late. I parked the ambulance at the side of the road. The bodies were taken to the previously decided location and dropped into the hollow (less sandbags of course). Shovels were used to cover them and the Padre said a short prayer. This it had to be, because I had spotted searchers coming over the horizon. They started work early. They were spread out and I was reminded of an enemy attack again on our trenches. We sped off down the road to Albert. What the searchers, who must have heard us and probably saw us, made of the party of four men and an ambulance at 6 or 7 o'clock in the morning I can't think, however scrutiny of the records of search in this particular area subsequently showed that three unknown bodies were recorded as recovered from the map reference at which we had deposited them.

Back we went to Albert where I found a French blacksmith who split my nut off for me and I was able to dry out the water/petrol mixture. What he thought we were doing at that time of the morning is not recorded. We got back to St. Pol about midday, a weary party.'

The extraordinary amount of detail which Major General Sir Cecil Smith included in his account paints an entirely believable picture. He addressed the St. Pol Cemetery reburial question, but interestingly he indicated that the matter of three graves suddenly appearing in the immediate aftermath of the operation, and the unwanted attention that they would have attracted, posed a problem for the authorities that required some thought. The rank-heavy make-up of the ambulance crew again adds weight to the theory that the entire operation was carried out by officers only, in order to maintain a high level of secrecy and eliminate any loose chat amongst the ranks and leaks to the hungry press. What then of Smith's 'live' passengers who accompanied him on that macabre journey in November 1920; The unnamed Lieutenant Colonel, Major Williams and the Chaplain, the Reverend George Standing? Were they at St. Pol when the Unknown Warrior was selected? Can we link them to Major-General Smith and the others whom we know took part?

Henry Williams was born in Howth, Dublin in 1897, his father, Newton Stannard Williams, came from Belfast and his mother was from County Westmeath in Ireland. Henry had two sisters and an older brother Newton Williams, who served during the Great War as an officer in the Gloucestershire Regiment and the South Persian Rifles, serving in Iran. Following the death of his father in 1907 Henry attended Christ's Hospital School in England. He left school in 1913 at the age of 16 and gained employment in the Westminster Bank. At the outbreak of war in 1914 Henry enlisted in the 28th battalion of The London Regiment, also known as the Artists Rifles. He was sent to France and quickly promoted to Corporal owing to his previous service in his school O.T.C. unit. It wasn't long however until he was discovered as being under age and sent back to England. While back home he was recommended for a cadetship and returned to France commissioned as a 2nd Lieutenant with the 1/4th London Regiment. In his obituary published in the *Daily Telegraph* on the 4th October 1993, which reflects closely an audio history account which he recorded for the Imperial War Museum in 1990 at age 93, it is reported that the idea of an Unknown Warrior was entirely his and that of Sir Fabian Ware. In either account nothing is mentioned of his ambulance journey after the selection of the body but he did state that he was 'responsible for choosing five unknown soldiers from different theatres of the First World War, one of whom was ferried across the channel to his final resting place in Westminster Abbey.' There is no doubt however that Williams was at St. Pol when the selection took place as he can be seen in the 'Ireland v The Rest of the World' Hockey team photograph alongside Ernest Fitzsimon and Cecil Smith, obviously having qualified for selection with his Irish birth. He can also be identified in the St. Pol D.G.R.&E. officers' group photograph. After service in the D.G.R.&E. He transferred into the newly established Imperial War Graves Commission on 29th July 1921 and served with them, on and off, between spells employed in the furniture trade until March 1947.

The Reverend George Standing C.B.E, D.S.O., M.C., the Chaplain who accompanied Cecil Smith and Henry Williams in the ambulance following the selection featured in the structure of the St. Pol D.G.R.&E. While not appearing in the 'Q Branch' list he was photographed with some of the aforementioned officers and also appears in the St. Pol group photograph along with Wyatt, Gell and the other identified officers. In an obituary following his death on the 6th January 1966 it is stated:[30]

> 'After the war ended, while serving in France, he was concerned with other officers in the secret procedure for the selection of the Unknown Warrior.'

Although a brief sentence, the reference to 'other officers' perhaps corroborates what has been suggested in that the operation was carried out by officers only. One interesting photograph, in which the Reverend Standing appears, part of the Fitzsimon archive, and replicated in the author's own collection, is of particular interest in light of Sir Cecil Smith's account. It shows, very clearly, the Reverend George Standing, a young Lieutenant Cecil Smith, Major Henry Williams and Major Ernest Fitzsimon. In a letter written to author Janine Watrin in November 1985 Sir Cecil Smith[31] stated that the photograph of him, accompanied by Williams and Standing, was of the three men who took part in, as he described, 'the midnight ride with the three unknown British soldiers'. He further stated that the man pictured on the right of the image, Major Fitzsimon, did not take part in the ambulance journey. This, although eliminating Fitz from actual involvement in that part of the operation, does indicate that he may have taken a planning role as outlined in his curriculum vitae. In attaching

---

30 Minutes of the Methodist Conference, Obituary G. Standing C.B.E. D.S.O. M.C. 1966.

31 Letter from Sir Cecil Smith to Janine Watrin dated 12th November 1988, Author's private collection.

credence to any of these accounts one always comes back to the differences concerning the date and the number of bodies selected. As has been highlighted the accepted start date, the date on which the bodies were selected, was set as the 7th November 1920 as a result of General Wyatt's definitive letter to the *Daily Telegraph* on 11th November 1939. To prove that the General was mistaken a more contemporaneous record would need to be found showing a different date.

The Imperial War Museum in London hold General L.J. Wyatt's personal papers. The file itself is not particularly large, consisting of a number of photographs attached to album pages showing exhumation units at work on the old battlefields. Others show scenes of cemeteries in France and Belgium when the graves were marked with wooden crosses such as Tyne Cot Cemetery near Ypres, where the original German bunkers can be seen and Polygon Wood Cemetery, also close to Ypres with its obelisk memorial prominent. Another series of images show the officers who attended the Amiens Australian memorial ceremony on the 7th November 1920 photographed as they made their way on foot from the Cathedral to the Hotel Du Rhin. In one image Major Fitzsimon can be seen, walking behind General Wyatt with Marshal Foch, a different view than the scenes captured in the Fitz-Simon archive images. A hard-backed book in the collection contains invitation acceptances from local French dignitaries who had been invited to a fete at British Army Headquarters in St. Pol on the 18th July 1920. On examining the documents I pulled from a large envelope a handwritten document titled 'The Unknown Warrior' along with a type-written transcript. The original handwritten document was dated the 28th November 1935 and was signed Brig. General L.J. Wyatt. In the account General Wyatt explained how the selection process had been left to him by the Adjutant General and that he decided the following:[32]

---

32 Imperial War Museum, L. J. Wyatt Private Papers, Catalogue Ref. 14122

'(a) The Body must be a British soldier, and that there could be no means of him being identified.

(b) A Body should be chosen from each of the four Big Battle Areas; Aisne, Somme, Arras and Ypres.

(c) The Bodies should be brought to my Hd. Qrs. at St. Pol and placed in the Chapel there on the 8th November 1920.

(d) The parties bringing the Body should at once return to their areas.'

So there was the confirmation that the generally accepted date was wrong, a mistake or perhaps a misquote or misprint. As if to cement the point General Wyatt goes on to state:[33]

'At 12 midnight 8/9th Nov, it was reported to me that the four bodies had arrived and accompanied by Lt. Col. Gell, one of my staff, I went to the Chapel.'

The point could not be clearer. The General went on to describe events later that day, the 9th November when the body was sent under escort in an ambulance to Boulogne and then on the 10th when it was taken to the Quayside where Marshal Foch and General Sir George Macdonogh, representing His Majesty The King, received it. The sequence of events from the 8th November until the operation entered its public overt phase flowed without the awkward gap or jump in the story. The selection of the body of the Unknown Warrior took place on the night of the 8th/9th November 1920; an important point to clarify when considering the remarkable contents of the next document examined.

33 Ibid.

6

Cagnicourt B.C.

MAJOR GENERAL SIR Cecil Smith's account of events following the selection of the body, as detailed as it was, took us to an unknown spot by the side of the Albert to Bapaume Road. He offered no explanation as to what actually happened to the three bodies hastily covered with earth in the path of the oncoming searchers. He stated that scrutiny of the relevant documents was later carried out to indicate that three bodies had been recovered from that specific area yet he did not state that he personally carried out that exercise. It is impossible to try to ascertain where on the road this spot might have been as the description, although basic, is misleading. The reconnaissance that was carried out at the point 'N.W.' indicating northwest along the road is impossible to even guess. The Albert to Bapaume Road, or D929 runs northeast in a straight line between Albert and Bapaume, cutting through the little villages of La Boisselle and Pozières where the British and German front lines crossed the road. Certainly in this general area there would have been an abundance of suitable locations to bury the remains in abandoned trench works or shell holes; the area definitely would have been devastated as he described, with ample opportunity for the Graves Registration Units to reinter the found remains in the nearby concentration cemeteries at either Gordon Dump or Pozières itself. The road does not however run northwest from Albert to Bapaume. The general area lies around 37 miles by road, south-east of St. Pol, a distance achievable by 4am as Smith had estimated, in a well-serviced contemporary vehicle leaving St. Pol shortly after the selection at midnight. The approximate location is certainly plausible but the north-west direction from the town of Albert is not. This final point in Cecil Smith's detailed recollection of events does not stand up to scrutiny.

Another aspect of his account deserves attention, the whole objective of this part of the operation was to discreetly re-inter the three bodies, a course of action that was deemed preferable to the sudden overnight appearance and detection of three fresh graves marked by crosses in a local military cemetery. Would the suspicion of the officer in charge of the searchers not be raised after the Graves Registration Unit discovered three sets of human remains loosely covered with earth in otherwise frozen ground? Especially if they had observed four men making away from the area in a British Army ambulance? Surely questions would have been asked. Does this mark the extent of Smith's knowledge of events? Or was there an element of subterfuge introduced to this part of his story to prevent the final details of the operation being compromised?

If young Lieutenant Cecil Smith was ordered to keep a secret then Major General Sir Cecil Smith was not going to be the man to leak it. Not even sixty years later at eighty-six years of age.

JACK FISHER

In late 2019 I began collaborating and exchanging information with film producers Jason Davidson and Pete Roch, who were interested in the Unknown Warrior story. They, like many before them, had wrestled with the inconsistencies in the different versions of the story that had been told over the years and were interested in the Fitzsimon material as it threw up a number of fresh sources of information to explore, notably from those lower ranking officers who could be identified in photographs as having played a part. Their assistance in identifying a number of those involved from unnamed photographs was invaluable. In December 2019, just a few days before Christmas, I was shown a number of documents by Jason and Pete relating to an officer who had commanded a Grave Registration Unit back in November 1920, Captain Albert John 'Jack' Fisher.

Albert Fisher, known as 'Jack' to family and friends, was born on the 21st August 1891 at Levenshulme in Manchester. Before the war he was employed as a clerk for an engineering company. In 1914, at the outbreak of war he enlisted in the 2nd Battalion of The Rifle Brigade and made a quick progression up the ranks, attaining Sergeant rank by 1917. In September 1917 he was commissioned as 2nd Lieutenant, remaining in The Rifle Brigade until the end of the war by which time he had been promoted again to Lieutenant. Following the Armistice Jack took up a position within the Department of Graves Registration and Enquiry (D.G.R.&E.) 'B' Branch, No.1 District, based at Duisans, east of Arras in France under the command of Major Reginald William Welfare Hills. On promotion to the rank of Captain on the 15th September 1920 Jack was appointed as officer in charge of Graves Registration Unit (G.R.U.) No.14, a unit of roughly platoon strength which worked along with G.R.U. No. 18, and another body recovery unit known as the 'Flying Squad' operating from the Duisans Camp, a base similar to St. Pol in that it had previously been used as a field hospital. Jack left the army in 1921 and found employment as a commercial traveller for the pharmaceutical industry. In his later years Jack moved to the Black Country where he lived with his son Gerald, daughter-in-law Kath and his granddaughter Sandra in Walsall. Jack passed away in 1985. Sandra remembers her grandfather as meticulous, straight thinking man who habitually sat in his favourite armchair and read a daily broadsheet newspaper with a large dictionary beside him. Occasionally he would stop reading and look up a word in the dictionary before continuing his daily read. He shared very few memories of his war service, in fact the only real detailed piece of evidence of his military service was not uncovered until after the death of his son, Gerald in 2007 some 22 years after Jack's death. On clearing out the contents of an old writing desk used by Jack, Sandra's late husband, Professor Christopher Hewitt, discovered a remarkable document that when read in context with the other relatively recently uncovered material, sheds a new light on the final resting place of the three unselected bodies in the Unknown Warrior Operation. Chris Hewitt, aware that he had uncovered something of historical significance, sent a copy of the document to the Black Country Bugle in which it was published on the 8th November 2007 along with a short covering story written by Chris. Chris' intention was that the item would be picked up on by historians who could have possibly placed it in context. That unfortunately did not happen and the document was deposited in the National Archives by Sandra Hewitt's mother in 2013. It is now held in the Westminster Abbey Muniments Collection where it was read by Jason Davidson and Pete Roch.

The main document was contained inside an envelope headed 'On His Majesty's Service' marked 'Secret' addressed to 'Capt. A. J. Fisher Comdg. GRU 14' which contained a handwritten letter also marked 'Secret' addressed to 'O.C. GRU 14' and headed 'CAGNICOURT B.C.' The heading meant nothing to me; initially I was confused by the 'B.C.' ending but as I read on this title became clear, meaning Cagnicourt British Cemetery. The main body read:[1]

> '1. Please arrange for a party of 4 French civilians, equipped
> with shovels for exhumation work, and an ambulance
> (capable of proceeding to St. Pol and back) to be at
> the a/n [above named] cemetery at 15.15hrs Nov 8th.

1 The National Archives, Albert Fisher, Captain, Military papers including letter rel. to Unknown Warrior, 1920, Acc 2013/002 Held by Westminster Abbey Library and Muniment Room.

You will personally see that they are there and hand them over on arrival to Lt. Col. N.G. Tronson Comndg No.1 District. Having done this you will return to your camp and stand by in case you are needed. The ambulance driver should be a French man also.

2. At 22.00hrs the same date you will again return to the cemetery with the French labour, equipped as before plus lanterns, and reinter in the cemetery 3 bodies (graves having been dug in the meantime). For this work again you will not be needed but will be required to stand by in your camp.

3. The contents of this document will not be communicated to anyone and you will arrange for the civilian labour yourself.

I will come and see you on Sunday to ensure all plans are satisfactory.

R.W.W. Hills.

Major. "B" No1 District

6/11/20

Copy to Col. Tronson.'

Was this the missing piece of the story? Firstly the date that the order was written on and the date that the orders were then to be carried out match what we now know the operation date to be. The order from Major Hills to Captain Fisher was issued on Saturday the 6th November 1920. Major Hills states that he would meet Fisher on Sunday, the following day which was the 7th November, the day when we now know Generals Wyatt, Macdonogh and Major Fitzsimon attended the Australian service at Amiens with Marshal Foch. The following day, the 8th November, Captain Fisher was to ensure three graves were dug in the late afternoon, at dusk, at Cagnicourt Cemetery, before returning to his camp at Duisans. Duisans is approximately 15 miles south-east of St. Pol on the road to Arras, half way to Cagnicourt. That night was the night General Wyatt stated in his 1935 account that the body of the Unknown Warrior was selected from four bodies brought to St. Pol, leaving three to be re-buried. Sir Cecil Smith then took up the story with his account aimed at correcting Reverend Collings in stating that the three bodies were buried at St. Pol, but in doing so continues to perpetuate Wyatt's mistaken date of the 7th November from the later 1939 *Daily Telegraph* account. So, it appears that on the night of the selection of the body of the Unknown Warrior, Captain Fisher was instructed to be at Cagnicourt Cemetery at 10pm and was specifically ordered to re-inter three bodies, in secret, by lantern light. Furthermore he was ordered to obtain French labour and a French ambulance driver to carry out the work with the ambulance being capable of making the journey to St. Pol and back; importantly only capable of making a journey of that distance, not specifically instructed to actually go there. Is this then the final resting place of the three men brought to St. Pol for selection?

The order paints an extraordinarily macabre picture of men digging on a dark November night under the yellow flickering light of hand held lanterns. The French civilian workers were undoubtedly chosen to ensure that there was no loose talk among the ranks, again cementing the theory that only officers were used in the operation. The geography does not add up, but then nor does the final piece of Sir Cecil Smith's account. St. Pol is roughly the same distance from Cagnicourt as Pozières, approximately 36 miles, Pozières being roughly half way between Albert and Bapaume. The distance from Cagnicourt to Pozières is about 19 miles. It appears we have knowledge of the beginning of the journey and the end of the journey but what happened in between is still unclear. Did Colonel Tronson simply rendezvous with Lieutenant Smith at the carefully reconnoitred grid reference and transfer the three bodies from one ambulance to the other? Or were the three bodies left as Smith described, loosely covered at the same spot to be recovered almost immediately by Tronson?

Were Colonel Tronson and his French crew the 'searchers' who Smith described as reminding him of a German attack advancing towards his position? Cecil Smith stated that they must have begun work early that morning, or was it the case that they had been out all night waiting for the broken down ambulance to arrive? There could be no advantage after all in a search team employed in body recovery work beginning their task early, at 6am on a morning in the darkness of a frozen November morning.

It is easy to speculate on matters unknown around this narrative; a number of points however can be corroborated as fact. The officer whom Captain Fisher was to meet with at Cagnicourt Cemetery, Lt. Colonel Norman Graham Piers De Coudray Tronson, was attached to the D.G.R.&E. at St. Pol at that time; indeed he also appears in the St. Pol group photograph along with the other main protagonists in the operation. He was not Captain Fisher's usual supervising officer. Lt. Colonel Tronson had served in the Boer War in the ranks with the East Surrey Regiment and was commissioned into the Leicestershire Regiment in October 1900. In the Great War he served with the North Staffordshire Regiment in the rank of Captain and ended the war temporarily attached to the Hampshire Regiment as Major before his appointment to the D.G.R. & E. at St. Pol. He died in July 1957 aged 81 years. The officer who issued the secret orders was however Captain Fisher's commanding officer and next in his chain of command, Major Reginald William Welfare Hills M.C. Hills also began his military career in the ranks with the Royal Fusiliers. He was commissioned in February 1915 and served in France from May of that year. In July 1916 he was appointed Lieutenant in the Royal Army Service Corps and had attained Captain rank by the end of the Great War. Major Hills was appointed Temporary Major attached to the Department of the Assistant Quartermaster General at Duisans in France from March 1920 until the 31st December

1920 when he left to take up a position in the Indian Army where he continued to serve during the Second World War achieving Lieutenant-Colonel rank. Hills was awarded the Military Cross in June 1918 and Mentioned in Despatches in December of that year, and was again Mentioned in Despatches in October 1939 and was awarded the O.B.E. on the 1st July 1941. He died in February 1962. So both these officers were attached to D.G.R.&E. Units at St. Pol and Duisans respectively, the chain of command indicated in the order was correct; the officers did exist, serving in roles and locations relevant to events.

Cagnicourt British Cemetery first began to be used from the 2nd September 1918 when the village was taken during the advance on the Drocourt-Queant German lines.[2] It was used for burials from that time until mid October 1918 and then contained 89 graves until it was enlarged after the Armistice and used as a concentration cemetery for reburials of graves found over a wide area around Cagnicourt. Today it contains the graves of 283 casualties, the majority of which are unidentified; 102 of these are identified First World War casualties and one grave dates from the Second World War. In November 1920 the cemetery fell within the boundary of the Duisans D.G.R.&E. unit. Documentation exists, held in the archive of the Commonwealth War Graves Commission (C.W.G.C.), relating to the exhumation and reburial of graves at Cagnicourt Cemetery in the form of Burial Returns which were completed and signed off by the officer in charge of each Grave Registration Unit who had been working there. These forms typically contain details of the burial plot number, the map reference of where the body was found, whether the original grave had been marked with a cross or not, the name and regiment of the soldier if known and the means by which the body was identified.

---

2 Commonwealth War Graves Commission, Cagnicourt B.C. https://www. cwgc.org/find-a-cemetery/cemetery/32501/cagnicourt-british-cemetery Accessed 7/4/2020.

On examination of these documents and consultation with the C.W.G.C. one thing was clear; there are no records of three unidentified burials having taken place on either the 8th or 9th November 1920. Similarly there are no cases of three bodies having been recovered together on either of those dates from one single map reference, let alone a map reference from the Albert–Bapaume Road area as indicated in Cecil Smith's letter. An examination of the Burial Return documents did however highlight some relevant information and a significant irregularity in grave positioning, that when looked at in conjunction with the other information relating to the cemetery and in the absence of an explanation, warrants some consideration.

Cagnicourt British Cemetery as we look at it today is located at the roadside of the D13 road that leads east from Cagnicourt village. It is sited close to the communal civilian cemetery; between the two there is a vacant space which once served as the location of a German cemetery, the graves having been removed some years ago. From the roadside the cemetery is laid out in three plots with Plot 2 closest to the road, Plot 1 at the centre and Plot 3 furthest away from the road. The vast majority of graves in Plot 3 were interred early in 1921 by members of G.R.U. 12 and 18 so for the purposes of explanation of events in November 1920 are not relevant. This is also the case for the majority of burials in Plot 1, rows C and B. On examining the documentation relating to the remaining graves it can be seen that burials took place on a pattern from left to right by date when viewed from the road and in rows from those furthest away towards those nearest the road. It can be seen that Captain Fisher, with G.R.U. 14, carried out reburials on the 6th October 1920 at Plot 1, row A graves 15 and 16,[3] which are at the right edge of the row.

3 Commonwealth War Graves Commission, Concentration Of Graves Burial Return, Cagnicourt British Cemetery dated 6th October 1920 Capt. A.J. Fisher. https://www.cwgc.org/find-war-dead/casualty/314155/claxton,-/#&gid=null&pid=1. Accessed 7/4/2020.

These were followed by four more burials in the same row, up to the right edge of the cemetery with the last taking place on the 20th October 1920. With the completion of that row one would expect burials to recommence after the 20th October at the left edge of Plot 2, row A. When we look at this row however we find that the first six graves were interred by Captain Leitch and G.R.U. 18 on the 20th November 1920 and are numbered, as one would expect, 1 to 6.[4] The next two graves however were interred by G.R.U. 14 Captain Fisher on the 10th November 1920,[5] a very relevant date, the next working day for Captain Fisher after the orders to secretly reinter three graves in this cemetery during the early hours of the 9th. If we then look at the burial return slip for the burials concerned we see that the first name is recorded as Pte. T. Renny 447196; the name recorded by C.W.G.C. is Rennie, not an unusual inaccuracy. The second burial is an unknown King's Regiment soldier. Further examination of the burial slip shows us that these two burials at plots 8 and 7 were initially designated as plots 1 and 2 by Captain Fisher and predate the six graves to their left. An alteration of Captain Fisher's original slip has been made in red. Rather than begin his reburial work at the left edge of the new row on the 10th November, he buried the two bodies in graves some distance towards the centre of the cemetery. Ten days later, on the 20th November 1920 Captain Leitch, the officer commanding G.R.U. 18, then sited six burials from the left boundary of the cemetery in Plot 2 row A up to where Captain Fisher's two plots were situated. Leitch's graves numbered 1 to 6 and the numbering of Captain Fisher's graves was altered

4 Commonwealth War Graves Commission, Concentration Of Graves Burial Return, Cagnicourt British Cemetery dated 20th November 1920 Capt. Leitch GRU 18. https://www.cwgc.org/find-war-dead/casualty/314166/davidson,-/#&gid=null&pid=1 Accessed 7/4/2020.

5 Commonwealth War Graves Commission, Concentration Of Graves Burial Return, Cagnicourt British Cemetery dated 10th November 1920 Capt. A.J. Fisher. https://www.cwgc.org/find-war-dead/casualty/314214/rennie,-/#&gis=null&pid=1. Accessed 7/4/2020.

from 2 and 1 to 7 and 8 respectively, completing a row. No marked grave in Cagnicourt Cemetery can be linked from the records available to an exhumation and reburial on the 9th November 1920. This then begs the question; if the operation planners were so concerned about three grave crosses suddenly appearing overnight, as indicated in Cecil Smith's narrative, were the graves then buried unmarked? If that were the case then no original crosses would have been erected to be replaced later with Portland stone headstones. There would be nothing today to mark the graves. Was it also the case that Captain Fisher's 10th November reburials were sited closer to the centre of the cemetery in an attempt to cover recent work in the vicinity? Then there would be a gap in the cemetery today close to the area in which G.R.U.14 were working, wide enough to have accommodated the three burials as indicated in the orders issued on the 6th November 1920. All of this hangs of course on whether or not the orders were actually carried out.

In considering that point I think we must look at Albert Fisher's subsequent actions. Firstly, the altered burial return relating to the burials at Plot 2, row A graves 8 and 7 was typewritten. Almost all of the other returns were handwritten. This indicates that Captain Fisher was meticulous with his record keeping or perhaps that this particular document was not prepared 'in the field' but afterwards in his quarters. A point to note on the form itself is a declaration added in the top right corner which states 'Certified crosses erected and checked A. Fisher (signature) Capt. O.C. G.R.U. 14'.

The most telling indication that the orders were actually carried out was the fact that they still exist; as secret orders they should probably have been destroyed. In a similar vein, if on the 7th November he had been told that they were cancelled, then why were they kept at all? They were instead retained by Jack Fisher, in the original envelope and never shown to or spoken of to anyone, even his family for as long as he lived; in fact they weren't even found until years after his death. The orders were unconventional to say the least, and probably questioned by Jack at the meeting with Major Hills on Sunday the 7th November. The meeting was obviously the forum in which any changes in timings or fine detail could be discussed but regardless of what assurances were made by Major Hills, Jack Fisher made a conscious decision to retain the document, to keep himself right should there be any future enquiry or questions asked as to why he carried out such an unorthodox clandestine burial. As the days passed he would have become aware of the press coverage of the Unknown Warrior burial at Westminster Abbey; by that time he probably realised that he had played a part in something very important and retained the order for a different reason, a point of pride. But did he still have a problem reconciling what happened on the night of the 8th/9th November? The answer to that question may be found in another document retained along with the secret orders. It was in the form of a reference dated 14th January 1921 and signed by Major Brown of No.1 District D.G.R.&E. At Duisans. Addressed 'To whom it may concern' it reads:[6]

> 'Captain A.J. Fisher has been employed under the Directorate of Graves Registration and Enquiries as O.C. Graves Registration Unit since 16th March 1919 to date. During this period he has had considerable experience in organisation of large working parties and particularly in general office routine.
>
> His reports and correspondence to these Headquarters have been exceptionally clear and good, and his office systems appears to be the result of sound business methods instituted by him.
>
> He is a very energetic and capable officer and I can thoroughly recommend him.'

---

6 The National Archives, Albert Fisher, Captain, Military papers including letter rel. to Unknown Warrior, 1920, Acc 2013/002 Held by Westminster Abbey Library and Muniment Room

The reference highlights the qualities which I had observed in examining the burial returns. Albert Fisher had fought through the Great War and advanced himself from Private to Captain rank. There is no doubt he was a good soldier and a leader; the reference Major Brown gave him was excellent. For a man to fight alongside and then lose colleagues, have them literally disappear without trace and without a grave and then to spend the best part of two years trying to find The Missing and recover what was left from the battlefield, was the last straw to bury three soldiers and leave their graves unmarked, regardless of the bigger picture? The answer to that question may lie in the final sentence of Major Brown's reference:

'He is leaving this sub-directorate at his own request.'

Jack Fisher relinquished his rank and left the army five days later on the 19th January 1921.

JIMMY SCOTT

After eight years my journey was over. I was led by the names in the little diary and found my way through the pain and suffering of the Great War from an over-crowded cottage in Tullyhue in County Armagh to the expanse of South Africa, to the mire of the Home Rule Crisis in Ireland and the hell of The Somme. My objective was never to write a book to tell the story of the Unknown Warrior, it was never to write a book at all, rather to preserve the remembrance of my great grandfather. The material left by Ernest Fitzsimon, 'Fitz' of 172 Roden Street, pushed me down a road from which there was no turning back, to tell a story that simply had to be told. The story of the Unknown Warrior, from its inception to its execution was nothing short of brilliant. The question of the fate of the bodies of the three soldiers not selected always left a bitter taste. To have been led to a position where I can highlight new evidence on the subject has been a troubling journey. I have presented this evidence well aware of the intense scrutiny that it will undoubtedly come under, and rightly so, the subject is an important piece of our National Heritage. I have attempted to penetrate the haze of time and to establish a narrative from the various accounts that are now available. My conclusion being that the bodies of the three men not chosen on the night of the 8th November 1920 were not discarded at the side of a road, nor was their discovery and burial left to chance, rather they received a proper burial in a British Cemetery alongside their brothers in arms. Indeed rather than having been referred to as the 'unselected unknowns' these three men served their nation beyond the grave by being part of an operation carried out in secret to preserve the remembrance of millions. By the touch of a General's hand their final resting place fell to chance; it was not to be among the kings at Westminster Abbey but nor was it in a ditch at the side of a French road. I believe that, based on my interpretation of the information I have examined, their final resting place is indeed at Cagnicourt British Cemetery, the exact spot concealed by the level of secrecy required to maintain the integrity of a brilliant operation, not against an enemy but to warm the hearts of a mourning nation. The plan was devised to ensure that no one person knew the details of the whole operation so we should not be so arrogant as to believe that we can disassemble it now. The Unknown Warrior was to be, and remains, just that, unknown. One contemporary and anonymous account of the final outcome of the operation, believed to be that of a British officer, epitomises what the Unknown Warrior meant to the people of Britain:[7]

'Thursday 11th Nov. 1920

The second anniversary of Armistice day, 1918. As, on that eventful day, the weather conditions were the best and the most fitting. I was able to reach Trafalgar Square about 10.30am and get right down to Whitehall and

---

7 Anonymous original account, courtesy of Michael Jackson, personal archive.

into the special reserved enclosure right opposite to the Cenotaph. Just before eleven as the November sun was piercing through the mist the massed bands of the Guards were heard up Whitehall. The King stood bareheaded and alone, a solitary figure as it were, facing Trafalgar Square. The procession came nearer, the arms of the troops lining the routes were reversed and presently, as it were, right out of the mist the Warrior of the battlefields came in his coffin on the gun carriage. The coffin draped with an old Union Jack from Ypres. The bands passed forward to the other side of the Cenotaph, the gun carriage bearing The Chosen of His Race swept right round across the roadway and halted in front of The King who stepped forward and placed a wreath by the side of the sword and "tin helmet" lying on the coffin. The pall bearers, leaders of renown in the Great War, took up their position and the moment now approached for the ceremonies in honour of the Dead to take place.

First, the massed bands played the hymn "Oh God our help in ages past" accompanied by the choir from St. Paul's Cathedral and joined by the congregation around. Then came the Lord's Prayer recited by all. As the clock struck the eleventh hour the King unveiled the Cenotaph and the two minutes silence was observed. At the end came the blast of "The Last Post", known to every soldier.

The Warrior passed on then to his last resting place in the old Abbey where he will remain the Ambassador to Britain of all those who died for her in the Great War.'

THEY BURIED HIM
AMONG THE KINGS
BECAUSE HE HAD DONE GOOD
TOWARD GOD
AND TOWARD HIS HOUSE

Epilogue
February 2020

THE MORNING WAS bright and crisp as once again I left Paris Charles De Gaulle airport and drove north into the French countryside. The first part of the journey at any rate was now a familiar one, judging distance between the many articulated lorries on the dull motorway as I attempted to learn the nuances of a strange hire car. My mind mulled over the events of the past eight years, the people I had met, many of them now friends, the places that I had been to, or more accurately been brought to by a list of names scribbled into a notebook. I thought of how those names resonated and had come to the fore when going about my day to day business.

A journey to Belfast was now a journey of remembrance as I passed otherwise everyday landmarks, hidden memorials of a distant age woven into the fabric of modern society. I recalled a journey that I had made the previous year, a journey from Comber, my home town, the final resting place of George Hackney, Ulster's finest war photographer, my great grandfather's friend and in many ways the man who sent me on this journey. To Comber Square and War Memorial nearby inscribed with the name of John McBratney, killed in action on the 6th May 1916, buried alive holding the front line at Thiepval Wood. Into Dundonald and on my left the final resting place of John Campbell, wounded in action within sight of the Y.C.V. flag, carried by his colleague, Brian Boyd on the 7th June 1917. John survived, long enough to be buried close to home after succumbing to his wounds a week after he was injured while being treated in a hospital in Dublin. I stopped in a heavy morning traffic shrouded in exhaust fumes, at Campbell College, and in my mind I paid respects to Jerome Walker who studied there in times of peace, oblivious to the violent end that awaited him also in Thiepval Wood. Moving on from the junction at Knock I glanced at the frontage of S.D. Bell's coffee shop. In 1912 Bell was a member of the founding committee member of the Young Citizen Volunteers. A century later his descendants became friends of my daughters, successfully making their way in life and studies at universities across the United Kingdom, representing a personification of my own personal definition of peace and freedom. The organisation he helped to form sworn to uphold the principles of non-sectarianism and non-politicalisation. Behind S.D. Bell's, the road leading to Ormiston House where the original Y.C.V.s paraded for photographs in 1913, among them Captain Charles McMaster MC who later led his trench mortar battery into action at Thiepval, taking the Schwaben Redoubt on the 1st July 1916 only to be lost a year later at Fretzenberg in Belgium without trace, one of The Missing. Half a mile further I made my way parallel to Cyprus Gardens, the home of young Brian Boyd, 10th Belfast Boy Scout and later Y.C.V. Battalion Scout, awarded the Military Medal for bravery at Thiepval and cut down, mortally wounded, the following year at Whytschaete, leading his battalion in Napoleonic style carrying the Y.C.V. flag aloft as the junior officer and ensign of a proud battalion of men. A few hundred yards later I was reminded again of Charles McMaster and his brother Lendrick as I passed Lendrick Street and then McMaster Street close to the end of the Newtownards Road where I turned left and then right, around St. George's Market, used for training and drilling the Y.C.V.s before the call of war.

Now, as the French countryside blurred past the car windows, I reflected on the purpose of that particular journey, to the British Broadcasting Corporation buildings at Ormeau

Avenue in Belfast City Centre. I recalled vividly being met at reception by Linda McAuley, the great-niece of Ernest Fitz-Simon. Linda led me into the building and into the main lift. There she handed me a bag, saying 'You carry these'. The lift stopped and I found myself in the BBC canteen on the top floor of the building. We were served coffee and walked to a free table surrounded by BBC staff. The bright sunlight cut through a row of windows and before sitting down at the table I realised, as I scanned across the rooftops of the terraced houses below, that I was looking south and 400 metres away was Elm Street, the street where my great grandfather Jimmy Scott had lived. I paused for a moment in thought. I imagined him making his way back and forth along Donegall Pass on a cold October in 1916, beginning and ending journeys with time short, honouring promises, as he ticked off the addresses in the small leather-bound book he held securely in his pocket. The book that I had held in a cold silent Authuile Cemetery seven years before. In my mind I gave a final respectful nod; I was there to finish his work, to see a job done. In my mind an important part of the journey had come full circle and one final piece had been put in place. I was about to witness the result.

Linda sat down and over coffee we chatted about John Fitz-Simon in Canada and what new discoveries I had made. She nodded to the bag that I was carrying; I had not realised that I had been holding what I had come to see. I opened the bag and lifted out three small hinged boxes and set each one carefully on the table before us. I opened them one at a time to reveal three medals, a British War Medal, a Victory Medal and a 1915 Star, each with their respective ribbon attached. The ribbons were clean and bright and the medals themselves sharp, sparkling and unblemished, reflecting brilliantly in the sunlight beaming into the canteen. I had seen many of these medals before but none so clean and sharp as these; they had been newly struck. I carefully prised the bronze Victory Medal from the recess in its box and lifted it up with its rainbow ribbon, admiring the perfect obverse engraving of the winged figure of 'Victory' or 'Victoria', with her left hand extended, holding a palm branch in her right hand. I turned the medal over and on the reverse read the inscription 'The Great War For Civilisation 1914-1919'. I thought again, as I had before, about the meaning of that simple sentence, those five words that preceded the dates, in particular the last two words, 'For Civilisation'. Those two words meant so much. Everything that had passed and all that will come to pass. All that we do in peace and freedom to live our lives. Civilisation.

I realised that the medals before me were not just Great War medals, discarded relics found in drawers and old shoeboxes; rather they represented values challenged since 1919, still upheld and under threat today. I thought about those words again as I turned the medal on its edge and read the details engraved there, '14604 Cpl J. H. Fitzsimons R. Ir. Rif.' I was holding Jack Fitzsimons' medal, issued in 2019, ninety-seven years after his mother refused to accept it, along with the other two of the set, way back in January 1922. Jeanie Fitzsimons understandably wanted her son, not three medals. Her refusal to accept them had been noted on the corresponding medal index card and the medals had been returned to Dublin for destruction. On receipt of documentation that I had forwarded to the Ministry of Defence via Linda, Jack's great-niece, the medals were restruck and sent to his family as if they had been newly issued.

I thought of how Ernest had struggled with his mother's refusal to accept Jack's death, as during his work with the D.G.R.&E. he made a point of visiting Connaught Cemetery at Thiepval, built in front of the little wood of the same name and within yards of the front line trench from where the men of the Ulster Division launched their attack on the 1st July 1916. There he searched for and found his brother's grave and had a photograph taken of him standing beside it which he then sent home as proof that Jack was indeed dead. I thought again of how important an actual grave is. Jeanie Fitzsimons continued to fight with her thoughts for years. I recalled how John Fitz-Simon had told me that not long after their marriage in 1928 Ernest and his wife Mabel were invited to a séance. Spiritualism had become increasingly popular in the wake of the Great War, when many people sought answers to the loss they had suffered outside of what the church at the time could offer. Ernest had little time for such matters but attended reluctantly and later told his son that the 'medium', after appearing to enter a trance, began to pull at her collar and called out 'Was Ernest there?' Ernest was startled as it was unusual for him to be referred to by his real name as opposed to just 'Fitz'. 'Ernest' was reserved for his siblings only. The medium went on to say, 'This is Jack, I've been trying to get in touch, tell Mother I'm all right, she's been worrying but I'm fine and now I'm moving on and will not contact you again.' Ernest knew that Jack hated wearing his military uniform as he felt constricted around his neck and constantly tugged at it, just as the medium had done. When the account of the séance was passed to his mother by Ernest she burst into tears and said, 'Oh, thank God. I've been worried sick about that boy, now I'll be easy.'

Over an hour passed driving at a constant speed along the monotonous French motorway route. I continued on past the exit that I would normally have taken to visit the Thiepval area, instead exiting at Bapaume, one of the towns mentioned in Major General Sir Cecil Williams account of the early hours of the 9th November 1920. On exiting I drove northeast towards Douai on much smaller rural country roads. Twenty minutes or so passed as I made my way through a number of rural, lifeless villages before I arrived at my final destination, Cagnicourt. I drove through the village until the houses and buildings on either side of the road disappeared and the countryside once again filled the car windscreen. Just at that point, beyond the edge of the village, a paved lay-by appeared on the right side of the road with the unmistakable Cross of Sacrifice marking the site of the Commonwealth War Graves Commission cemetery. I parked up and walked towards the little cemetery, stepped over the heavy chain and bollard boundary, and stood beside the great cross. My eyes scanned the front row of graves and almost immediately met a name made familiar to me through my research; the grave of Captain Sidney Cowan of the Royal Flying Corps. Sidney was born in Downpatrick in County Down, not far from my home town. A young Royal Flying Corps pilot, he was reported as missing in action following a mid-air collision over enemy lines on the 17th November 1916. In May 1917 a British officer who knew him from his time at Marlborough College discovered his grave some 12 miles south-east of Arras. The *Irish Weekly Times* carried the story on the 5th May 1917[1] when extracts of a letter from the officer who found the grave were published. Sidney Cowan's body had been buried by German soldiers in a grave with a rail surround marked with a cross which bore the inscription in German: 'In memory of a gallant English officer, Captain S.E. Cowan, killed in air combat 17th November 1916.' Captain Cowan's grave was not officially recovered until February 1921 when his body was finally laid to rest at Cagnicourt British Cemetery[2]. As I read the headstone and the additional inscription carved at the bottom of the stone: 'Also in memory of his brother Captain P.C. Cowan R.F.C. 8th November 1917, age 22'. I recalled that his brother Philip, also a flyer, was killed and listed as missing. The single grave marked the lives of two brothers lost. I pondered again on such a loss to a family. Sidney was only 19 years old when he

1 *Irish Weekly Times*, 'Distinguished Dublin Airman' 5th May 1917.
2 C.W.G.C Burial Return, Cagnicourt B.C. https://www.cwgc.org/find-war-dead/casualty/cowan,-sidney-edward/#&gid=null&pid=1 accessed 7/4/2020.

was killed yet he was a pilot of Captain rank and had been awarded the Military Cross on three occasions.

I walked slowly past Cowan's grave and found myself standing just to the right of where Captain Albert Fisher had buried the two graves on the morning of the 10th November 1920, initially numbered as 2 and 1 of the row and now most definitely numbered 7 and 8. At this point I stopped and looked at the next row of headstones, I put my hand into my jacket pocket and felt the mottled leather cover of Jimmy Scott's notebook; the journey it had sent me on was over. At the end of the third row of graves I found what I had been looking for; nothing, an empty space. I paused and bowed my head for a moment then turned and walked the few steps to the wall beside The Great Cross. There I opened the metal cabinet door and removed the cemetery register. I opened the book and commenced a new entry; beside the date and in the column next to my name I wrote three words:

'Known Unto God'

Acknowledgements

THIS PROJECT HAS hovered in the background of my life for almost eight years now. I am grateful to so many individuals and organisations for their assistance along the way. My grateful thanks to Robert McFarlane in facilitating my initial contact with the Fitzsimon family ultimately leading to my contact with Dr. John Fitz-Simon and Linda McAuley MBE whose contributions have been both fascinating and invaluable.

I must also thank the following for their assistance and expertise: The curator of the Royal Ulster Rifles Museum, Gavin Glass MBE and his staff and volunteers; Carol Walker MBE, Director of The Somme Association; General Sir Roger Wheeler GCB, CBE; The Commonwealth War Graves Commission; The National Army Museum; Ben Reiss, Morton Photography Curator, The National Trust for Scotland; Jamie Barron, Collections Care, Brodie Castle; The Imperial War Museum, London; The National Archive; Westminster Abbey Archive; Marc Glorieux, Friends of The In Flanders Fields Museum, Ypres and The Reverend Nicholas Pnematicatos.

I would like to thank the following for their willingness in sharing family information relating to persons mentioned in this book. Their contribution, often a shred of information passed down through family circles, preserved the remembrance of those mentioned in a unique and personal way: Judith Martin; Gary Gray; James George; Hughie Walker; The late Dave Donatelli; Deborah Weston and James McMaster.

My thanks also to local researchers who in the early days of researching this project were kind enough to point me in the right direction: Pat Geary, Lisburn; Nigel Henderson, County Down; Mike Jackson; Walter Millar and John McCormick from The Shankill Road in Belfast.

Special thanks to Malcolm Johnston and Jacky Hawkes of Colourpoint/Blackstaff Press.

Thank you to Patricia Fawcett for her support and unenviable work in proofing my work.

To producers Pete Roch and Jason Davidson of Squeaky Pedal Productions for their collaboration and willingness to share information.

To Sandra Hewitt for her willingness to share memories of her grandfather, Captain Albert Fisher and research carried out by her late husband, Professor Christopher Hewitt.

To Stéphane Watrin, Paris, for kindly passing on valuable documents, possessions of his late mother Madame Janine Watrin who tragically passed away on the 24th May 2020.

Finally, a very special thank you to my wife, Kim and my daughters Kathryn and Lauren for their patience and valued opinion. To Kim for being with me at the end, in Cagnicout British Cemetery, on the 31st January 2020.